Natural
Wonders
—— *of* ——
Ohio

Natural
Wonders
— of —
Ohio

A Guide to
Parks, Preserves
& Wild Places

Janet Groene and Gordon Groene

Illustrated by Dawn L. Nelson

Country Roads Press
CASTINE • MAINE

Natural Wonders of Ohio

Published by Country Roads Press
P.O. Box 286, Lower Main Street
Castine, Maine 04421

Text and cover design by Studio 3, Ellsworth, Maine.
Cover photograph courtesy of the Ohio Division of Travel and
  Tourism, © Terry Cartwright.
Illustrations by Dawn L. Nelson.
Typesetting by Typeworks, Belfast, Maine.

Library of Congress Cataloging-in-Publication Data

Groene, Janet.
    Natural wonders of Ohio : a guide to parks, preserves, and open
spaces / authors, Janet and Gordon Groene ; illustrator, Dawn L.
Nelson.
        p.   cm.
    Includes bibliographical references and index.
    ISBN 1-56626-053-1 : $9.95
    1. Ohio – Guidebooks.   2. Natural areas – Ohio – Guidebooks.
    3. Parks – Ohio – Guidebooks.   4. Gardens – Ohio – Guidebooks.
    5. Natural history – Ohio – Guidebooks.   I. Groene, Gordon.
    II. Title.
    F489.3.G77   1994
    917.7104'43 – dc20   93-41108
                                                                    CIP

Printed in the United States of America.
10 9 8 7 6 5 4 3 2 1

To Albert C. Andrews, Jr.,
who, as a newspaperman with the Berea News
and then the Cleveland Plain Dealer,
has been a mentor and friend.

Contents

Acknowledgments

Special thanks to Continental Airlines; Christine Zust and the Greater Cleveland Convention and Visitors Bureau; the Ohio Department of Natural Resources; Timothy Moore of the Ohio Division of Travel and Tourism; Cindy Schillaci of the Greene County Convention and Visitors Bureau; Kim Sheets of the Ohio Valley Visitor Center in Gallipolis; Deborah Herman and Mildred Brown of the Warren County Convention and Visitors Bureau; Shelly Horvath of Our House; and Lois Smith and the Greater Cincinnati Convention and Visitors Bureau.

Thanks, too, to Helen Dunlap and Dee Grossman of the Tuscarawas County Convention and Visitors Bureau; Joan Tims of the Youngstown/Mahoning County Convention and Visitors Bureau; Shirley McCallister of the Zanesville/Muskingum County Convention and Visitors Bureau; Carol Layh of the Lafayette Hotel in Marietta; Sondra Wagner of the Akron/Summit Convention and Visitors Bureau; James Rahtz of the Hamilton County Park District; Melinda Huntley of the Erie County Convention and Visitors Bureau; Lesley Ruskowski of Firelands College; Michelle Mueller of the Ottawa County

Visitors Bureau; Don Taylor of the Hocking County Tourism Association; Debbie Highman of the Monroe County Tourism Council; Mike Logan of the Pickaway County Visitors Bureau; Teresa Carper of the Ross-Chillicothe Convention and Visitors Bureau; Todd Wilson of Ohio Wesleyan University; Howard Hintz of the Buckeye Trail Association; and Comair, the Delta Connection.

Introduction

Ohio, our home state, was at one time a shameful symbol of industrial blight. Lake Erie was dead; the Cuyahoga River caught fire. Comedians cackled. The word *Cleveland* was always good for a snicker; *Youngstown* rated a guffaw. Then Ohio cleaned up its rivers, cleared its air, expanded its greenswards, and is having the last laugh.

Today the Buckeye State is a triumph of parks and preserves, woodlands and meadows, lakes and streams. Much work remains to be done, but it's being shouldered by vigorous, informed people who love and revere the state and are willing to work hard to restore it.

The Lake Erie shoreline is a glittering garland across the top of the state. Wave-lapped beaches, woodsy cabins, historic lighthouses, and picturesque fishing villages can still be found along the mainland and even more so on the Lake Erie islands. Ohio is where the Great Plains begin and the Ohio River rings almost the entire state. From East Liverpool all the way to Cincinnati, Ohio's border is wide and flowing water. Wayne

National Forest spreads across a vast area in southern Ohio, where the Appalachian Mountains touch the state.

Forgotten seas, vanished rivers, and glaciers of unimaginable power have shaped the land and coursed underground to form massive caves. In more modern times, canals and railbeds were hacked through virgin forests, which are now being returned to nature.

Just as we found when we were writing *Country Roads of Ohio* (Country Roads Press, 1993), a book about Ohio's green spaces can cover only a fraction of the natural wealth to be found in this gentle state. Yes, there are great cities, gritty and gray, but most of the state remains clothed in the green of fields and forests and in the blue of sweet water.

Ohio's state parks alone can fill a book—and do. *Ohio State Parks* by Art Weber (Glovebox Guidebooks, 1993) has 383 pages. And that covers *only* the state parks, not the many city and county parks, state recreation areas, state nature preserves, wildlife reserves, national scenic sites, and countless gardens and arboretums that are operated by universities or other private groups.

We are all the richer for having lived in Ohio, but all the poorer for having to choose only some of the choicest morsels from this feast to serve up in this book. So we ask that you start with these pages and then continue to explore, write for information, ask questions, and add your list of favorite green spaces to ours.

How to Use This Book
To find most of these sites, you'll need a good map. They aren't tourist attractions, blared about on billboards. Many of them aren't shown prominently in road signs or tourist brochures. If possible, write well in advance to the site itself, and call Ohio State Tourism, 800-BUCKEYE, with your requests for supporting

information about motels, campgrounds, festivals, canoeing, spelunking, wildflowers, and all your other special interests. The Ohio state map is available free from tourist authorities at the toll-free number above, but it's best to get maps that are even more detailed. Sometimes they are available free from county and regional authorities, but we especially recommend the *Ohio Gazetteer,* published by the DeLorme Mapping Company and available in bookstores.

It goes without saying that no specimens of any kind should be collected in the parks and reserves we list. Plants, fossils, minerals and rocks, and animals are all protected. If you want to know whether you can take a bicycle, motorized vehicle, or leashed pet, or do anything in the green space except walk and look, phone ahead. In general, the "Leave No Trace" policy applies.

Unless noted otherwise, all sites listed in this book are free and are open during daylight hours. Observe these hours carefully because in some cases the gates or the parking area are locked at sundown, and you could find yourself or your car locked in.

General Information

All-Terrain Vehicles (ATVs)
If you drive any sort of ATV, including four-wheel drive (4WD), get advance information about where these vehicles can and can't be used. They are excluded from some wilderness areas, including Ohio Power's ReCreation Land, and welcomed in others.

Bicycling
The 314-mile Cardinal Trail crosses central Ohio through North Canton, Canal Fulton, Hayesville, Fredricktown, Prospect, West Liberty, St. Paris, New Middletown, and New Paris. It is marked every 5 miles and at turns. Marked bicycle routes also run from Cincinnati to Maumee (239 miles), Cincinnati to Marietta (240 miles), Cincinnati to Cleveland (294 miles), Portsmouth to Toledo (494 miles), Marietta to Conneaut (244 miles), McGill to Mifflin (a 156-mile route that connects Indiana with the Cardinal Trail), and McGill to Pierpont (300 miles). These routes are on public (but scenic and little-traveled) roads and are not to be confused with bikeways and bike paths that are not open to vehicular traffic. A 24-mile bikeway extends the 24 miles from Dayton to

Miamisburg along the Great Miami and Stillwater rivers. Much of the route is on bicycles-only paths; some is on public roads.

Bicycling is enormously popular in Ohio, home of the Wright brothers, whose bicycle shop can still be seen in Dayton. The state has many local, regional, and statewide bicycle routes, mountain bike outings and races, and other events for two-wheelers. Call 800-BUCKEYE and ask for brochures on biking Ohio. When writing individual tourism bureaus, specify your special interest in bicycling.

Boating

Request brochures from the Division of Watercraft, 1952 Belcher Drive, Building C-2, Columbus, OH 43224-1386; 614-265-6480. Brochures are published by region, so if you have a destination in mind, indicate it.

Camping

A call to 800-BUCKEYE will bring you a campground and visitors guide, plus any other Ohio tourism literature you need. However, the campground guide is also available for $2 via first-class mail if you're in a hurry. Send a check to the Ohio Campground Owners Association, 3386 Snouffer Road, Columbus, OH 43235.

Through the Rent-a-Camp program, which is available in many of Ohio's state parks, novice campers can give camping a try without making a big investment in equipment. Set up and maintained by professional park staff, each campsite contains a ten-by-twelve-foot tent with a dining canopy, two cots with sleeping pads, a cooler, a propane camp stove, a lantern, a broom, a dustpan, and a doormat. Bring your own food, ice, bedding, and personal gear.

Fishing

Everyone over the age of sixteen who fishes anywhere in Ohio must have a license. Exceptions are attendants for fishermen who are handicapped (only one line permitted for both persons), fishing in private ponds, and members of the armed forces who are on annual leave. Licenses are available to persons age sixty-six and older, persons who are physically disabled and require assistance to fish, residents of state and county institutions, holders of "Veteran" license plates, permanently disabled vets, and former prisoners of war.

Ohio residents may buy annual licenses at a preferred rate; others may buy an annual or three-day nonresident license.

Forests

For information about Ohio state forests, contact the Division of Forestry, Fountain Square, Columbus, OH 43224; 614-265-6694.

Golf

The following Ohio state parks have golf courses:

	Yards	Par	Pro Shop
Deer Creek	7,134	72	614-869-3088
Hueston Woods	7,005	72	513-523-8081
Maumee Bay	6,941	72	419-836-9009
Punderson	6,825	72	216-564-5465
Salt Fork	6,056	71	614-432-7185
Shawnee	6,837	72	614-858-6681

Nature Preserves

For information about state nature preserves that are open to the public, contact the Division of Natural Areas and Preserves, Building F, Fountain Square, Columbus, OH 43224; 614-265-6453.

Pets

About half of the campgrounds in Ohio state parks permit

camping with pets. Generally, pets are not permitted in arboretums and other private green spaces. Always phone ahead.

Life Histories

Brochures on the life history in Ohio of the following species are
available from the Department of Natural Resources Publications
Center, 4383 Fountain Square Drive, Columbus, OH 43224.
The first ten on your order are free; send $1 postage for each
additional ten or fewer items. Keep in mind that the brochures
listed below accent the *Ohio* life of the species, even though
many of them live part of their life cycles elsewhere.

American Crow
American Eel
Bald Eagle
Barn Owl
Beaver
Bigmouth Buffalow
Black Crappie
Bluntnose and Northern
    Fathead Minnows
Bowfin
Brook Trout
Brown Stileback
Brown Trout
Bullheads
Canada Goose
Cardinal
Carp
Central Johnny Darter
Central Longear Sunfish
Central Mottled Sculpin
Central Quillback
Channel Catfish
Coho Salmon

Common Bobwhite
Common Shiner, Common
    Emerald Shiner
Common White Sucker
Eastern Bluebird
Eastern Burbot
Eastern Cottontail Rabbit
Eastern Fox Squirrel
Eastern Gray Squirrel
Eastern Screech Owl
Flathead Catfish
Freshwater Drum
Gizzard Shad
Golden Redhorse
Golden Shiner
Gray Fox
Great Horned Own
Green Sunfish, Warmouth
Lake Sturgeon
Lake Whitefish
Least Brook Lamprey, Silver
    Lamprey
Longnose Gar

Long-tailed Weasel
Mink
Mooneye and Goldeye
Mosquitofish
Mourning Dove
Muskellunge
Muskrat
Northern Bluegill
Northern Largemouth Bass
Northern Pike
Northern Rock Bass
Northern Smallmouth Bass
Nutria
Opossum
Paddlefish
Pickerel
Pumpkinseed
Raccoon
Rainbow Smelt

Red Fox
Ring-necked Pheasant
Ruffed Grouse
Sauger
Saugeye
Skipjack Herring
Southern Redbelly Dace
Stonecat
Striped Skunk
Walleye, Blue Pike
Whistling Swan
White Bass
White Crappie
White-tailed Deer
Wild Turkey
Wood Duck
Woodchuck
Woodcock
Yellow Perch

Available at the same terms and from the same address listed above are brochures describing all the wildlife found in the following state wildlife areas:

Auburn Marsh
B & N Coal, Inc.
Beaver Creek
Berlin Lake
Big Island
Brush Creek
Caesar Creek
Conesville Coal Lands
Cooper Hollow
Darke Wildlife Area
Deer Creek

Delaware Wildlife Area
Dillon
East Fork Wildlife Area
Fallsville
Fox Lake
Grand River
Hambden Orchard
Highlandtown
Indian Creek
Kaul Wildlife Area
Killbuck Marsh

Killdeer Plains
Kokosing Lake
Lake La Su An
Liberty Wildlife Area
Little Portage
Magee Marsh
Mercer
Metzger
Milan Wildlife Area
Mohican River
Montie Lake
Mosquito Creek
New Lyme
Oldaker
Orwell
Oxbow Lake
Paint Creek
Peabody Coal Company
Pickerel Creek
Pleasant Valley
Powelson Wildlife Area
Resthaven
Ross Lake
Rush Run

Salt Fork
Shawnee State Forest
Shenango
Shreve Lake
Spencer Wildlife Area
Spring Valley
Sunday Creek
Toussaint Wildlife Area
Tranquility Wildlife Area
Trimble Wildlife Area
Tycoon Lake
Waterloo
Wellington
Wellston
Wildcat Hollow Primitive
    Weapons Deer Hunting
    Area
Willard Marsh
Willow Point
Wolf Creek
Woodbury
Wyandot Wildlife Area
Zepernick Lake

These Ohio state parks have restaurants, meeting rooms, and guest rooms or cabins for overnight guests:

Burr Oak   614-767-2112
Deer Creek   614-869-2020
Hueston Woods   513-523-6381
Maumee Bay   419-836-1466
Mohican   419-938-5411; cabins, 419-994-4290
Punderson   216-564-9144

Salt Fork   614-439-2751
Shawnee   614-858-6621

About the Buckeye Trail
A 1,200-mile hiking trail loops the entire state of Ohio, threading through forty of the state's eighty-eight counties. Blue blazes mark the main trail; side and alternate trails are blazed in white. The trail is about 75 percent original and about 25 percent shared with other trails, including some township roads. By writing the Buckeye Trail Association, Box 254, Worthington, OH 43085, you can become an individual or family member and order waterproof section maps that show the trail route, public roads, towns, campsites, water supplies, and points of interest.

To walk the trail from Lake Erie to Cincinnati is an achievement. To hike its entire loop length is not only a personal triumph but also a unique and in-depth way to see a state whose gifts of nature, culture, and heritage are beyond measure.

Were you to start the loop in Lake County, your trek would take you south through the Tuscarawas Valley and Amish country into the Belle Valley and rugged hills. The trail turns west at Morgan County through moonshine and coal mine country and into the Hocking Hills. At Adams County in southern Ohio, it jogs south to where early iron foundries were the foundation of what later became a thriving steel industry.

The trail nips a corner of Hamilton County to avoid bumping into Cincinnati, wends north through Warren County and Caesar Creek, then continues north along the old Miami and Erie Canal path to the historic Black Swamp area and along the meandering Maumee River.

Turning back east, the trail gives Lake Erie a wide berth, preferring instead to ride the rich ridges through farm fields and fruit trees into Medina County, with its Norman Rockwell villages, and across the Cuyahoga Valley to the starting point on the lake.

The Ohio to Erie Trail

Like the Buckeye Trail, this 320-mile trail is a massive undertaking for both its promoters and its users. To cover the trail, you start in Cleveland and go down the Cuyahoga Valley. The trail passes through New Philadelphia, Coshocton, Newark, the Columbus area, London, Springfield, Xenia, and Lebanon, ending in Cincinnati. Unlike the Buckeye Trail, which is a hiking trail, this one is accessible to walkers, people in wheelchairs, bicyclists, skiers, snowmobilers, and, in some areas, horseback riders. Most of it follows old rail rights-of-way and the towpath of the Ohio and Erie Canal, which in some sections still contains water.

In rural areas, the trail is eight feet wide and has a fine gravel surface. In other areas, it's as wide as ten feet and paved.

For more information, write or call Ohio to Erie Trail, Box 14384, Columbus, OH 43220; 614-262-1001. This is a volunteer effort, so if you call, you'll probably get an answering machine.

Junior Naturalists

Many of the state parks offer summer nature programs. A child who attends three sessions of the Naturalist Aide Program receives an arm badge.

Ohio state parks have no admission fees, but fees may be charged for other services such as camping, electric hookups, or admissions to special park features.

1

East-Central Ohio

Nimishillen, Conotton, Tuscarawas, Sandy. Strung together, the words sound like a football cheer, but they're actually the names of rivers and creeks that form the skeins on which east-central Ohio is strung.

America was still a British colony when Moravian missionaries made their way to a forested Eden along the Tuscarawas River, taught Christianity to the Indians there, and joined them in creating a colony. The year was 1772, more than two decades before there would be a Cleveland.

The settlement at Schoenbrunn, and a later experiment at Zoar, were doomed to disappear into the mists of history until later generations brought replicas of them back to life. Today the land along the Tuscarawas is a mecca for history hunters, but they also have plenty of allure for the traveler in search of unspoiled fields and forests, creeks and reservoirs.

CANOEING THE TUSCARAWAS

The 130-mile Tuscarawas can be canoed all year, as can a large network of connected creeks and rivers, including the 23.5-mile Walhonding River, 81.7-mile Killbuck Creek, 41.3-mile Sandy Creek, and 92.2-mile Wills Creek. Sugar Creek, which joins the Tuscarawas north of New Philadelphia, can be canoed seasonally. They're all Class 1 canoeing waters, languid and relaxing.

From a starting point at Carlisle Canoe Center in New Philadelphia, the thirty miles to Newcomerstown can be paddled in about ten hours. Or canoe the fifty miles to Coshocton in seventeen hours. The route takes you through some of the state's best history and scenery, including the picture-book village of Gnadenhutten (locally pronounced "jah-NAY-den-hutten").

Where: Southeast of town on State 416 at the river.
For more information:
    Carlisle Canoe Center, 1567 State 416 S.E., New Philadelphia, OH 44663. 216-339-4010.

THE ZOAR VALLEY TRAIL

Fort Laurens, built in 1778, was the only Revolutionary War fort in Ohio. Now a pleasant picnic area with a museum and a crypt containing the bodies of twenty-one soldiers who died defending the fort, it's one terminus of the seventeen-mile Zoar Valley Trail, which ends at Schoenbrunn Village. Established as a German commune in 1817, the village of Zoar has eight buildings operated for the public by the Ohio Historical Society.

Part of the 1,200-mile Buckeye Trail, this portion follows the towpath of the Ohio and Erie Canal. You'll pass the descendants of giant sycamores that, in ancient times, could sleep up to twenty travelers at a time. The hollows of today's younger trees are home to small forest animals.

Hikers can spend the night at Camp Tuscazoar, with its

rugged hills and valleys and views of Dover Dam and the Tuscarawas Valley. A stagecoach trail once passed the site, which was originally owned by the Zoarite settlers.

At the Schoenbrunn end, you'll find a green and pleasant log cabin village made up of seventeen reconstructed buildings, planted fields, and the original pioneer cemetery. It's open daily during the summer and on weekends only in the fall.

Where: Zoar Village is three miles southeast of exit 93 off I-77 on State 212.

For more information:
Tuscarawas County Convention and Visitors Bureau, 101 East High Avenue, P.O. Box 926, New Philadelphia, OH 44663. 216-364-5453 or 800-527-3387.

THE MUSKINGUM LAKES

Draw a circle roughly fifty miles in diameter around Canton, and you're in a wonderland of lakes formed by the Muskingum Watershed Conservancy District. All are bordered by public lands, ranging in width from a thin strip to hundreds of feet. Ten lakes add up to 16,000 acres of water surface, 3,000 tent and trailer campsites, countless cabins, 10 marinas, 38,000 acres of wooded hills and valleys, and a complete resort on Atwood Lake. Here we'll look at just a few of them. Others are listed in Chapter 12 and Chapter 13. Also in the system are small and un-developed Beach City Lake, northwest of New Philadelphia, and Wills Creek Lake, southwest of New Philadelphia. Both have launch ramps but no other facilities.

For more information:
Muskingum Watershed Conservancy District, Box 349, New Philadelphia, OH 44663. 216-343-6647.

Atwood Lake

Atwood Lake allows outboard motors up to 25 horsepower, but this is a sailor's lake, where weekend sailboats spread a show of billowing white across the wavelets. If you're not a rag sailor, watch the show from a rented pontoon. Or canoe around the 28 miles of shoreline, enjoying 1,540 acres of water that is as deep as 41 feet in places.

Where: Atwood Lake is west of Carrollton, eleven miles southeast of exit 93 off I-77 on State 212. The park entrance is on County 114. Atwood Lake Resort is on the south side of the lake on State 542.

Facilities: Cottages, picnicking, rest rooms, playground, observation towers, nature center, rangers, organized activities, sandy beach, hiking trails, marinas, boat launch, airstrip, campground. Atwood Lake Resort has fine dining, golf, indoor and outdoor pools, tennis, exercise and whirlpool facilities, and 104 hotel rooms and 17 shoreline cabins that accommodate up to 10 people.

For more information:

Atwood Lake Resort and Conference Center, 2650 Lodge Road, Dellroy, OH 44602. 800-362-6406.

Atwood Lake Park, 216-343-6780.

Clendening Lake

Clendening Lake, west of Cadiz in lightly populated Harrison County, is one of the less developed of the lakes. Most of the park's 4,750 acres are in a natural state, and only a few access points are provided. The 1,800-acre man-made lake was created in 1937 by damming Brushy Fork Creek. Outboard motors must be 10 horsepower or less.

Where: The lake is two miles north of Freeport and ten miles southeast of Uhrichsville on State 800. A free launch ramp is found on County 6.

Facilities: Camping, free launch ramps, marina, rest rooms, swimming area.
For more information:
Marina, 614-658-3691.
Campground, 614-658-3691.

Leesville Lake

Leesville Lake, just below Atwood Lake, is best known for its record-setting muskies, but anglers also catch their limit of other fish, including bass, bluegill, walleye, and channel catfish. Boat the thousand acres of water, but don't bring a kicker larger than 10 horsepower.

Where: Leesville Lake is east of Sherrodsville, just north of State 164.
Facilities: Marinas, rest rooms, launch ramps, playground, camping. The picnic area is near the dam.
For more information:
Marinas, 216-627-4270 (Northfork) and 614-269-5371 (Southfork).

Piedmont Lake

Piedmont Lake, in the northwest corner of Belmont County, is stocked with the most popular fishing species, and hidden in the surrounding hills are rustic cabins and campsites. Outboard motors must be under 10 horsepower. Roam the 4,372 acres of conservancy land or boat the 2,270-acre reservoir. See what's going on in the amphitheater, take hikes on the nature trails, and then light a charcoal fire and grill the day's catch.

Where: Piedmont Lake is about twenty-three miles west of Wheeling, West Virginia, and fourteen miles south of Cadiz, off US 22.
Facilities: Motel, cabins, campsites, marina with food service,

A white-footed mouse scrubs up after dinner

boat rentals, launch ramps, rest rooms, picnic facilities, activity center, sandy beach with changing rooms, launch ramp, amphitheater, nearby airstrip, nature programs and hikes led by a trained naturalist.

For more information:
Marina, 614-658-3735.

Tappan Lake
Tappan Lake, southeast of New Philadelphia, is a huge broth of powerboats, sailboats, canoes, pedal boats, and pontoons spreading for miles along the south edge of US 250. Fishermen come to catch bass, walleye, and other popular fish.

Where: Southeast of Dennison, off US 250.

Facilities: Restaurant overlooking the lake, free launch ramps, marina, cabins, picnic area with grills, concession stand, rest rooms, sandy beach with lifeguard and changing rooms, bumper and pedal boat rental, miniature golf, amphitheater, nature hikes with the park naturalist, programs, hiking trails, convenience store, laundry, game room.

For more information:
Campground, 614-922-3649.
Cabins, 216-343-6647.
Marina, 614-264-2031.

LIBERTY SEED COMPANY

Here's a chance for gardeners to see a seed catalog come to life. The Liberty Seed Company's trial gardens next to the Trumpet in the Land amphitheater in New Philadelphia are open from mid-July through September. The seed store, "plant alley," and the greenhouse are open from April to mid-June.

Where: Off I-77, take West High Street into downtown New Philadelphia. At the square, it becomes East High Street. Continue half a block, then turn right at Michael's Restaurant into an alley. At the four-way stop sign, you'll see Liberty Seed on your right. Be sure to call to see if it's open.

For more information:
Liberty Seed Company, 128 First Drive S.E., New Philadelphia, OH 44663. 216-364-1611.

EAGLE CREEK STATE NATURE PRESERVE

Snakes and salamanders, spotted turtles and opossums thrive in this swampy wetland. Migratory birds, including Canada geese and blue herons, stop at the ponds that were created here by hospitable beavers. The 441-acre preserve is home to foxes, deer, raccoons, hawks, and owls. Tall trees surround rich peat lowlands that put on a show of wildflowers from early spring through hard frost.

Where: Two miles northeast of Garrettsville on Center Road, then south on Hopkins Road.
Facilities: Observation blind, 300-foot boardwalk, 5 miles of hiking trails.
For more information:
   Eagle Creek State Nature Preserve, 614-265-6453.

CANTON GARDEN CENTER

Perhaps because Canton's native son President William McKinley was also assassinated, the city seemed to suffer special pain when President John F. Kennedy was killed in 1963. The JFK memorial fountain and continuous flame in the Canton Garden Center are part of the loveliness of these acres of spring bulbs, summer annuals, and a crescendo of late-summer color when the mums begin to bloom. When the peony bushes bloom in late May and early June, the perfume is intoxicating. People who are deaf or blind will enjoy the five-senses garden.

Where: Stadium Park, 1615 Stadium Park N.W., Canton.
Facilities: Picnic tables, grills, drinking water, rest rooms. Also in the Stadium Park complex are the Pro Football Hall of Fame and the majestic McKinley National Memorial, which has a sweeping view of the city.
For more information:
   Canton Garden Center, 1615 Stadium Park N.W., Canton, OH 44700. 216-455-6172 or 216-489-3015.
   Pro Football Hall of Fame, 2121 George Halas Drive N.W., Canton, OH 44700. 216-456-8207.

2

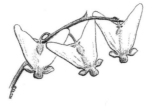

Little Miami River Valley

Just as the Cuyahoga Valley has been restored from an industrial wasteland to a recreational bonanza, the Little Miami River has been transformed into a silvery sword sheathed in green Ohio parklands. Along most of its length is a bicycling and walking trail. The river itself is a canoe trail that can be followed (with portages around dams) from Clifton to the Ohio River.

Almost the entire riverfront is a city or state park, a nature preserve, a forest reserve, or another green space. The trip downstream begins in a thin, meandering creek that moves into a towering gorge and gradually widens as it threads through 300-foot bluffs to reach floodplains as wide as two to three miles. Only two centuries ago, Indian villages lined these banks. Daniel Boone lived here, both as an explorer and as a prisoner of the Shawnee Indians.

With the pioneers came gristmills, dams, and all the other development that grew along rivers in early America. Today the remnants of these civilizations, from the Hopewell culture in

300 B.C. to nineteenth-century factories, provide some of the state's most interesting history-hopping for the Little Miami hiker and canoeist.

Most of the river can be paddled year-round, although it's always wise to consult local experts. Winter is the crystal, quiet time that locals like best. The water turns a greenish blue, mirroring the white bark of the stark sycamores. Snow piles plumply on the riverbanks, and icicles cling to walls of the gorges, but the water flows on, rarely freezing, searching for spring.

With springtime come wildflowers, waves of migrating birds, and leafy greenery. Summer brings the crowds, of course, but it also brings the scent of honeysuckle and the flutter of hummingbirds. Fall straggles in late, but its colors are worth waiting for. Canoe outfitters offer pig roasts and hayrides to keep the fun alive as the season wanes. Foxes and squirrels burrow in for the winter; raccoons raid more boldly; migratory birds flee. And the cycle begins again.

CLIFTON GORGE NATIONAL NATURAL LANDMARK

Clifton Gorge cuts a canyon through the dolomite of the Niagara Escarpment in a dramatic vision of the glacial and postglacial havoc that occurred here eons ago. Time healed the scraped, scarred land and carpeted it with 347 species of wildflowers and 105 species of trees and shrubs—including some wildly alien plants that are native to the far north. They were dropped here by glaciers millennia ago, and somehow they survived.

It is at the gorge's Narrows that a legend was born. Daniel Boone, who had been captured by the Indians, is said to have jumped to freedom across the gorge. Although there is some dispute about whether it was Boone or another member of his party and whether the twenty-two-foot leap could have been made at all, it's an intriguing tale to ponder while you explore the preserve. Waves of pioneers were drawn to the area by the Little Miami River, first as a means of transportation and then to use the power of its flow as a source of energy. Dozens of mills dotted the area. Clifton Mill, which remains, is one of the best and most beautiful of Ohio's remaining mills.

The old Pittsburgh-Cincinnati stagecoach route followed the Little Miami River in this area. An overgrown foundation along the Orton Memorial Trail is thought to be the remains of a brick inn that served stagecoach passengers. The North Rim Trail is another footpath, which follows the cliffs and offers awesome views of the gorge. The North Gorge Trail passes Amphitheater Falls and views Steamboat Rock. It's especially spectacular when spring wildflowers are in bloom.

The walking trails are in the "interpretive" preserve on the north side of the river. The much larger scientific preserve on the south side of the gorge remains in a natural state and can be entered only with a permit.

The preserve borders John Bryan State Park, which has more hiking trails plus swimming, picnicking, and a campground. The park also borders Antioch University's Glen Helen Nature Preserve (see next entry).

Where: In northeast Greene County on State 343, one-quarter mile west of Clifton on the east side of John Bryan State Park.
Facilities: In addition to four miles of challenging trails, the preserve has rest rooms. John Bryan State Park has many more facilities.
For more information:
Clifton Gorge State Preserve, Jackson Street, Clifton, OH 45316. 513-964-8794.
John Bryan State Park, 3790 State 370, Yellow Springs, OH 45387. 513-767-1274.

ANTIOCH UNIVERSITY'S
GLEN HELEN NATURE PRESERVE

Operated by Antioch University, this private preserve covers 1,000 acres of woods and waters. Visitors are welcome to hike 20 miles of scenic trails and to visit the Raptor Center and the Trailside Museum.

Facilities: Museum, trails, rest rooms. Adjacent to John Bryan State Park (see previous entry), with camping, picnic areas, and much more.

For more information:
Glen Helen Nature Preserve, 405 Corry Street, Yellow Springs, OH 45387. 513-767-7375.

CAESAR CREEK STATE PARK
and CAESAR CREEK GORGE STATE PRESERVE

Layers of bedrock heaved and rose during some unknown eruption eons ago, forming the ridge known as the Cincinnati Arch and exposing some of the oldest rocks in the Midwest. Here in the sedimentary limestone and shale, fossils show the kinds of life that thrived here in some long-vanished sea.

Geological formations along the 180-foot-deep Caesar Creek Gorge present a constantly changing panorama as the sun passes over and shadows change. Above it, gentle hills are covered with oak, hickory, beech, and maple trees, providing a home for deer, raccoons, red foxes, and box turtles. Red-tailed hawks soar overhead in an aerial ballet, searching for small prey.

Where: Caesar Creek State Park is located ten miles south of Xenia and Dayton. From I-71 go north on State 73 to the park office. Caesar Creek Gorge State Preserve is three miles north of Oregonia on Corwin Road.

Facilities: Like so many of Ohio's green places, Caesar Creek State Park is filled with picnic areas, 38 miles of hiking trails, boat access, a beach on Caesar Creek Lake, a village of log cabins, an interpretive center, campsites, 35 miles of bridle trails, and a camp for riders. The 463-acre Caesar Creek Gorge State Preserve is less developed, offering only rest rooms and marked trails.

For more information:
Caesar Creek State Park, 8570 State 73 East, Waynesville, OH 45068. 513-897-3055.
Caesar Creek Gorge State Preserve, 513-932-2347.

NARROWS RESERVE

Operated by Greene County, this sliver of a park follows the Little Miami River for about a mile. At the Upper Narrows, you'll find an interpretive center, canoe launch area, rest rooms, and three hiking trails—one of them along an abandoned asphalt road that is being reclaimed by the forest, another that follows the ridge of the valley. The River Trail runs the length of the reserve and ends at the Lower Narrows.

At the Middle Narrows, hikers and canoeists will see towering sycamores and deep, calm pools in the river. At the Lower Narrows, you can pick up the Big Woods Trail, which winds through centuries-old oaks; the newer Sugar Bush Trail, where you'll stumble upon an old steam engine rusting in a ravine; the sunny Meadow Trail, which features captivating wildflowers; and the Cold Springs Trail, which rambles past old homesites.

Where: Take US 35 to Factory Road, then go south to Indian Ripple Road.

A gray squirrel dines on an acorn

Facilities: Canoe launch, hiking trails, interpretive center, rest rooms.

For more information:

Narrows Reserve Interpretive Center, 2575 Indian Ripple Road, Beavercreek, OH 45430. 513-429-9590.

Greene County Park District, 651 Dayton-Xenia Road, Xenia, OH 45385. 513-376-7445.

MORROW TO MILFORD

Hiking, bicycling, or canoeing the river trail over the twenty-two miles between Morrow and Milford starts at milepost 22.5, where you'll see the Morrow Train Station, built to serve a railroad that arrived here in 1844. Giant sycamores shade your passage through the area known as the Deerfield Gorge, and suddenly an enormous factory looms into view. It's the Peters Cartridge Company, which at press time was looking for tenants.

This huge industrial complex had its own waterworks and generating plant and as many as 5,000 employees. Most of the old munitions factory has now been reclaimed by the dense forest. Molten lead was dropped from its soaring shot tower to form shot used in two world wars. The factory can be seen from the river at milepost 15.5.

A low dam at the Foster Viaduct at milepost 12.5 provided power to an important gristmill located here a century ago. You'll soon pass waving stands of a stout green reed known as scouring rush. It's so rough that pioneers planted it to use for cleaning pots and pans.

The Loveland Train Station at milepost 8.5 was built in 1906 by the Baltimore and Ohio Railroad. Today it's an art gallery and also has bicycles for rent. At milepost 2, you'll pass the old Camp Dennison School, dating to 1870. A half mile later, note the Secrest Monument. It's a tribute to the 75,000 Union troops who trained at Camp Dennison during the Civil War. The trail ends at milepost 0.0 at the Milford Train Station, which served the Little Miami Railroad, one of Ohio's first rail lines. The station dates to 1840.

Where: This stretch of the trail starts at Morrow on US 22.

Facilities: Rest rooms at Morrow, Glenn Island, Loveland, and Lake Isabella (entry fee); bicycle rental at Loveland; picnic shelters at Glenn Island and Kelley Preserve; picnic tables at Loveland; canoe access points at Hall's Creek, Glenn Island, Lake Isabella (fee), Rahe Preserve, and Milford.

Canoeing: Canoe outfitting is available through Morgan's Livery, located at Fort Ancient State Memorial on the Little Miami River, and in Springfield on the Mad River (which flows into the Great Miami). For more information, call 800-932-2663. Canoe rental in Loveland is available at Bruce's, 200 Taylor Street, 513-683-4611 or 513-683-4604. RiversEdge Canoe Livery and Outfitters is located on US 42 between Xenia and Waynesville, 513-862-4260.

For more information:

Little Miami, Inc., 3012 Section Road, Cincinnati, OH 45237. 513-351-6400.

Warren County Convention and Visitors Bureau, 777 Columbus Avenue, Lebanon, OH 45036. 800-433-1072.

NATURE'S BOUNTY

Apples, juicy berries, luscious sweet corn, glistening eggplant, crisp green beans, field-ripened tomatoes, homemade pastries. It's impossible to drive Warren County without stopping at the farms and roadside stands to gorge on freshly squeezed juice and stock up on fresh produce, homemade preserves, and home-baked pies and breads. For a free map showing the locations of farms that belong to the Warren County Fruit and Vegetable Growers Association, call 800-433-1072.

3

Licking River Valley

NEWARK EARTHWORKS

The Hopewell Indians felt the spell of the Licking River so
strongly that they chose the present site of Newark, where the
North Fork and South Fork join to form the main branch of the
Licking River, to build the most massive group of earthworks of
this type in the United States.

Today the Newark Earthworks form an impressive four-
square-mile complex that makes a superb weekend ramble as you
try to imagine why, in the years A.D. 100 to 500, tons of dirt
were moved by primitive methods to form these enclosures.
Today we can only guess at their social or ceremonial uses.

First visit Mound Builders State Memorial, where the sixty-
six-acre Great Circle surrounded a burial site with walls as high
as fourteen feet. A museum on the grounds contains pottery
shards, copper trinkets, bones, shells, and beads found when the
site was excavated. A small admission is charged.

East of this memorial at the Wright Earthworks, another
one-hundred-foot wall fragment can be seen. Octagon Earthworks

State Memorial encompasses another fifty acres, which borders a twenty-acre site whose meaning has been lost over time. Admission to all is free.

Don't miss Flint Ridge State Memorial, an ancient quarry where Indians found flint for their tools and arrowheads. Walk the trails, have a picnic, and visit the museum. Admission is charged.

Where: Mound Builders State Memorial is at South Twenty-first Street at Cooper, Newark. Wright Earthworks is at James and Waldo streets, Newark. Octagon State Memorial is at North Thirtieth Street at Parkview, Newark. Flint Ridge State Memorial is five miles east of Newark on State 16, then five miles south on State 668. The Licking County Convention and Visitors Bureau is located at 50 West Locust Street, Newark.

Hours: The museums are open Wednesday through Sunday, Memorial Day through Labor Day. Limited hours apply at other times of the year. Phone ahead.

Facilities: Rest rooms at all sites. The memorials have picnic sites. Flint Ridge has special trails for people with physical or visual impairments.

For more information:
Licking County Convention and Visitors Bureau, Box 702, Newark, OH 43055. 702-345-8224.

Exploring the Valley
The main channel of the Licking River and several miles of the North Fork are canoeable year-round. Many other stretches of the North and South forks also are accessible. For information, request Boating on Ohio's Streams, Section 4 (Southeast), from the Division of Watercraft, 1952 Belcher Drive, Building C-2, Columbus, OH 43224-1386, 614-265-6480.

A 14.5-mile bicycle trail begins in Newark on Cherry Valley Road, just north of West Main Street and just south of State

16. It passes through the picturesque villages of Granville and Alexandria. The Buckeye Central Scenic Railroad also offers special excursions through the county.

HEBRON STATE FISH HATCHERY

Few states can boast a better fisheries management program than Ohio. Moreover, the wildlife experts who operate the state's fish hatcheries make the whole process educational and entertaining as well. Water to operate the 60 acres of ponds that hatch about 3.5 million fish here each year are drawn from Buckeye Lake through the old Ohio and Erie Canal. More than 240 species of birds, including a long list of shorebirds, have been spotted on this 217-acre preserve since 1958. Make it a point to stop to see the hatching and rearing ponds and to sweep around with your binoculars to view the bird life.

Where: Two miles southwest of Hebron on Canal Road.
Facilities: Nature trails.
For more information:
    Hebron State Fish Hatchery, 614-928-8092.

BUCKEYE LAKE STATE PARK

Once a great glacial swamp, this area was flooded in 1825 to form a reservoir that was used to regulate water levels in the Ohio and Erie Canal between Carroll and Granville. A massive man-made ditch, the canal ran 333 miles from Lake Erie to the Ohio River and contained 152 locks. The coming of the railroads put an end to the canal era, the reservoir was abandoned, and Buckeye Lake took shape. For a time before and during World War II, it was more an amusement park than a green space. But the honky-tonks left, and only the park, with its landmark lake, remains.

The lake's Cranberry Island is a relic of the postglacial era, when plants that the glacier had caught up in Michigan and Canada were deposited here. Indians once gathered cranberries in the bogs. The island, which is found near the north shore of the lake, is a National Natural Landmark covered with plants normally found farther north.

Bird-watchers are well rewarded with sightings of upland birds and waterfowl, and picnickers can set up under big cottonwood trees.

Where: East of Columbus, south of Newark, and west of Zanesville. The east end of the lake is reached from State 13, the north shore from State 79, and the west and south from State 37. The park office is at the southwest end of the lake on Liebs Island Road. The route to the park entrance is well marked.

Hours: The park is open daily from 6:00 A.M. to 11:00 P.M.

Facilities: Boating with unlimited horsepower, beaches, snowmobiling and ice fishing, fee and free launch ramps, a variety of picnic areas, waterskiing areas, good bird watching for both waterfowl and upland species. Although this is a popular park year-round, flush toilets and some other facilities are unavailable in winter.

Special note: Cranberry Island is being eaten away by the wake of passing boats and is shrinking dramatically. Visitors are not permitted to go ashore except for one day each year, when they can stroll the boardwalks over the spongy moss island.

For more information:
Buckeye Lake State Park, 614-467-2690.

DAWES ARBORETUM

During a trip to England early in this century, Beman Dawes saw a tree that a soldier had planted to commemorate his safe return from the Battle of Waterloo. The idea had such a sense of permanence and tradition that Dawes started it here even before this arboretum in Newark was formalized. He invited the rich and famous of the day to plant trees here and added plaques honoring them. Trees planted by John Glenn, Gene Tunney, General John Pershing, Wiley Post, and other luminaries form the core of one of the Midwest's most important collections.

Come often to observe the ever-changing landscape in different seasons. Arrive early in the day to stroll the 355 acres on miles of footpaths. (You can also drive through to see the highlights of the arboretum. The speed limit on the 2.5-mile paved trail, which has two short side loops of one-half and one mile each, is 15 mph.)

Every inch of land has been used to its best advantage for the nature lover. A swampy area cradles one of the northernmost plantings of bald cypress. Walk the boardwalk for a close look at trees that can live to be centuries old and grow a hundred feet around. The swamp is especially lively in spring, when it's filled with frogs and fairy shrimp. As the season warms, it dries up, and its busy wildlife population quiets down.

Move on to the Shade Garden, where ferns and wildflowers nestle softly under a canopy of sheltering trees. You'll soon stumble upon a pioneer cemetery dating to 1813 or earlier. It's named for John Beard and Benjamin Green, Revolutionary War veterans who were the area's first settlers.

Take the path into the Deep Woods, all that remains of the beech-maple climax forest that greeted Ohio's first white settlers. Opposite it is a maple collection that is clothed in gaudy color each autumn, as well as rare trees such as the paperbark maple, lacebark pine, and Japanese Stewartia.

At the corner of the property in the pine collection, climb an observation tower to view the entire arboretum, including the famous hedge that spells out "Dawes Arboretum." One of the largest lettered hedges in the world, it is 2,040 feet long with letters 145 feet high, all sculpted out of plantings of a low-growing shrub. From the tower, you also have a grand view of Dawes

Lake. This 8.5-acre man-made pond attracts a surprising number of migratory waterfowl in spring and fall.

Leaving the pond, you'll walk through a stately arch of street trees, flanked by a crab apple garden that is a fairyland of pink and white in spring and a cornucopia of fragrant fruit in fall. It's a working tree garden, where scientists are evaluating species for disease resistance.

Emerging from Pershing Avenue, as the line of street trees is called, look for the buckeye trees planted to form the number seventeen. They are in honor of Ohio's entry into the Union as the seventeenth state.

The path continues on through a collection of oaks from around the world, a holly garden containing more than 100 species of deciduous and evergreen hollies, and into the Prairie Garden, where ancient grasses are being planted and preserved.

The three-acre Japanese Garden is one of the arboretum's special spots. It dates to 1964, when it was designed by Makoto Nakamura, a landscape architect at the University of Kyoto. True to its intention, it's not a flower garden but a triumph of total landscaping design in all its colors, forms, and subtleties.

The All Season Garden near the entrance also glows with color from early spring through the last icy breaths of fall.

Save the hot afternoon hours for two indoor tours. The Visitors Center houses one of the finest bonsai collections in the Midwest. A Scotch pine in the display is thought to have originated in 1910; an exquisite ginkgo dates to 1935. From a bay window in the Visitors Center, you also have a good view of the Bird-Watching Garden, where fountains, feeders, and plants have been selected to attract birds. The area is also visible from an outdoor stadium north of the center.

The arboretum's second indoor attraction is the original Daweswood House, built in 1867 with an exterior of handmade bricks and a native sandstone foundation. Indoors, climb the semicircular walnut staircase to the second floor, where thirteen-foot ceilings help keep the home cool in summer. After seeing the home, visit the peaceful Dawes Memorial, where the benefactors of this Eden are buried in an imposing Vermont granite mausoleum.

Now meander back along the Tree Dedicators Trail (mentioned above), the original arboretum that was planted with sugar maples in 1917, and the Park Woods, with its majestic maples and, in springtime, stunning rhododendrons.

Where: Five miles south of Newark on State 13.

Hours: The grounds are open from dawn to dusk every day except Thanksgiving, Christmas, and New Year's Day, when weather conditions permit. The Visitors Center is open weekdays, 8:00 to 11:30 A.M. and 12:30 to 5:00 P.M.; Saturday, 9:00 to 11:30 A.M. and 12:30 to 5:00 P.M.; Sunday and holidays, 1:00 to 5:00 P.M. During January and February, the center is closed Sunday.

Special note: If you'd like to see a computerized list of the collection at Dawes Arboretum, set your modem as follows: baud rate, 300 or 1200; parity, none; stop bit, 1; length, 8; full duplex; handshaking inbound and outbound. Call 614-323-4058 twenty-four hours a day. When a carrier is detected, press Enter two times. At the password prompt, type TAXON and press Enter. Instructions on the screen will guide you through the plant list.

For more information:

Dawes Arboretum, 7770 Jacksontown Road S.E., Newark, OH 43055. 614-323-2355 or 800-44-DAWES.

DILLON STATE PARK

Black Hand sandstone, sculpted through the centuries by wind and water, forms the gentle hills and wide valleys that make up this park, which lies on the western edge of the Allegheny

Plateau. Sand, worn from mountains that were located in the East millions of years ago, accumulated in a massive delta that covered much of what is today southeastern Ohio. The sand, packed and pressured as it grew deeper, became sandstone.

Throughout the park, you'll see outcroppings of this distinctive rock. One exposed rock, located twelve miles from the park, looked like a human hand blackened with soot. Because it appeared to point to nearby Flint Ridge, it was thought to be an ancient guide, put there for Indians in search of flint. The petroglyph is only legend today, as it was destroyed in 1828 during the digging of the Ohio and Erie Canal.

Flowing through the sandstone, the Licking River was dammed to provide hydropower to an early settlement and iron foundry. The present reservoir, the recreational core of the park, was built for flood control in the 1960s.

Deer, grouse, quail, pheasant, squirrels, and rabbits roam the 5,888-acre park and can often be seen along the hiking trails. The three-quarter-mile Ruffed Grouse Trail was designed to show the variety of habitats throughout the park. It's a branch of the 6-mile Licking Bend Trail, which follows the lakeshore. Other side trails are Blackberry Ridge, 1 mile; King Ridge Loop, 1⅛ miles; and Hickory Grove Loop, 1.5 miles.

Waterfowl sightings are frequent, especially colonies of egrets and herons, migratory birds in the autumn, and wild turkeys, which were introduced for fall hunting.

Where: Northwest of Zanesville on State 146.
Facilities: Amphitheater with stories and other campfire programs on weekends, part-time naturalist, rest rooms and latrines, camping, changing booths, concessions, boat launch and docks, seven miles of hiking trails, boat rentals, camp commissary.
For more information:
Dillon State Park, 5265 Dillon Hills Drive, Nashport, OH 43830. Park office, 614-453-4377. Camp office, 614-453-0442.

BLACKHAND GORGE STATE NATURE PRESERVE

Only ten miles from Dillon State Park and geologically part of it, this small preserve has even more appeal for hikers and day-trippers than the park itself. A dashingly beautiful slit in the sandstone formations, the gorge follows the Licking River.

One legend says that the gorge marked the boundary of a sacred Indian no-man's-land that was shared by all. No hand could be raised in anger against another. All tribes, depending equally on flint for tools, arrowheads, and firestarters, shared equally in the wealth of this lode.

The gorge's trails are lined with leafy woods on one side and breathtaking views of the river on the other. On the heights, mountain laurel and oak, hickory, and pine trees thrive; on the slopes and ravines is a mix of hardwoods; and the moist lowlands host sycamores, cottonwoods, box elders, and willows.

Remains of the Ohio and Erie Canal can be found here and there, as can old trolley tunnels that remain from the interurban railway. Like most of Ohio's green spaces, the preserve is especially beautiful during spring wildflower bloom and when autumn color is at its peak.

Where: Ten miles northwest of Dillon State Park on County 273; go eight miles east of Newark on State 16, then a quarter mile southeast on State 146 and 1.5 miles south on County 273.
Facilities: Hiking trails, paved paths for bicycles and wheelchairs, latrine, well, interpretive walks (call ahead or check bulletin boards).
Canoeing: The gorge can be seen by kayak or canoe. The Licking River is rated Class 1.
Special note: The 4.5-mile bicycle path in Blackhand Gorge is the first section of the paved 110-mile North Central Bikeway, which will eventually extend from Mount Gilead southeast to McConnelsville.

For more information:
Blackhand Gorge State Nature Preserve, 614-265-6452.

THE WILDS

It may be a shock to see gazelles and zebras loping across Ohio fields, but this 9,154-acre preserve between Cumberland and Chandlersville is an event. The largest animal preserve in the world (according to its supporters), it encompasses rolling grasslands, dense forests, and 150 lakes. The preserve supports a wildlife population that includes wild horses, red wolves, Hartmann Mountain zebras, scimitar-horned oryx, Przewalski's Asian wild horses, and Cuvier's gazelles.

A former strip-mined wasteland, the acreage has been fenced in, laced with dirt roads, and supplied with a small visitors center. For now, the center is concerned more with preservation than with tourism, but limited tourist visits are welcomed. At present, you can go to the visitors center, which is situated at the highest point, and look out over the land, but animals may not be in view. Work is proceeding slowly as funds become available, and it is hoped that safaris through the refuge will be offered.

Where: Southeast of Zanesville. Don't go, however, without calling ahead to ask for directions and visiting hours.
For more information:
The Wilds, 85 East Gay Street, Suite 603, Columbus, OH 43215. 614-228-0402.

4

Mahoning River Valley

MILL CREEK PARK

One of the oldest metropolitan parks in the state, this 2,530-acre park in Youngstown grew up around Mill Creek at the point where it enters the Mahoning River. It was named, we assume, for the many mills that sprouted in this area at the dawn of the industrial age. In its green embrace today are twenty-one miles of drives and fifteen miles of footpaths, three major lakes, ponds, forests, meadows, bold outcroppings of sandstone, and the gorge created by the creek itself.

One of the mills, the third flour mill built on this site, remains. The land was originally owned by John Young, founder of Youngstown, who sold it in 1797 to the builders of the first mill. The mill you see today was built by German Lanterman in 1845–46. It fell into disuse and became part of the park in 1892. By 1933, part of it was used as a museum.

The site also has a covered bridge, and just downstream

you'll find the Gorge Trail Boardwalk. It makes a loop of about two miles through beautiful gorge and waterfall scenery. Before you go, stop at the mill gift shop to pick up a brochure, which explains the self-guided tour.

Schedule at least half a day to tour Fellows Riverside Gardens at the north edge of the park. The rose collections are splendid, blooming from early summer until the first freeze. Modern roses are shown in a formal setting, but climbing roses and other old favorites abound throughout the gardens.

The view of Youngstown from the Great Terrace shows the city in all its industrial might and blight. Once one of the filthiest of northern Ohio's rust belt cities, Youngstown is slowly cleaning itself up and coming back.

Walk the herb garden, the rhododendron garden, and the winding paths of the rock garden. On hot days, take refuge in the Victorian gazebo, with its daylilies and peonies, in the shade garden, or under the beech trees at the north end of the Great Lawn.

Springtime along Mill Creek and the Mahoning River features 50,000 bulbs—crocuses, tulips, and narcissi. Don't miss the Daffodil Meadow, which is part of the park. To reach the meadow, go two miles south on Glenwood Road, then take Newport Drive along Lake Newport.

Where: Take the Belle Vista exit off I-680, then head south, following the signs to Mill Creek Park.
Hours: Lanterman's Mill is open Tuesday through Sunday from May through October. For information, call 216-740-7115. The Fellows Riverside Gardens are open from 10:00 A.M. until dark Monday through Friday; from April through mid-December, the gardens also are open from noon to 4:00 P.M. on Saturday and from 1:00 to 5:00 P.M. on Sunday. For information, call 216-792-7961.
Admission: The park is free, but some facilities have fees.

Facilities: Rest rooms are located throughout the park's "people" areas and gardens. Many areas are wheelchair accessible, and the park offers excellent drive-through sight-seeing for people with physical disabilities. Other facilities include picnic tables, grills, ice-skating, supervised playgrounds, a volleyball court, baseball diamonds, tennis courts, fishing in two lakes, the Pioneer Pavilion with a woolen mill, and the historic flour mill open for tours.

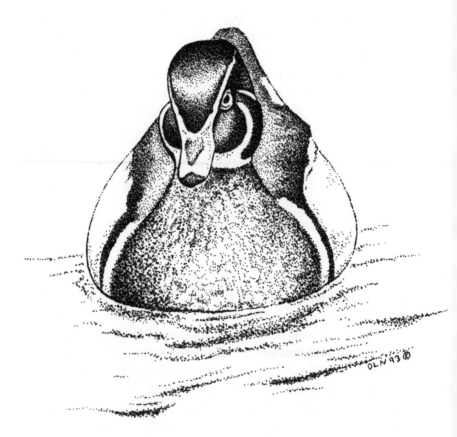

A magnificent male wood duck

For more information:
    Mill Creek Park, 816 Glenwood Avenue, Youngstown, OH 44502. 216-743-PARK.

KYLE WOODS STATE NATURE PRESERVE

A greenbelt that splits off Mill Creek Park to follow Indian Run, Kyle Woods is an eighty-two-acre state nature preserve that has the same terrain and wildlife as the park but fewer visitors because there are no facilities. Birds and other wild creatures, seemingly oblivious to the rushing cars and trucks on the turnpike, go about their feeding and nesting while observers snap photographs, make notes, and enjoy the private show.

Where: From Canfield, take US 224 east 1.5 miles to Tippecanoe Road. Turn south onto Tippecanoe Road, go a half mile, and then turn west onto the turnpike access road. The preserve is just south of the Tippecanoe overpass.

For more information:
    Kyle Woods State Nature Preserve, 216-527-5118.

BEAVER CREEK STATE PARK

South of the shepherd's crook formed by the Mahoning River in an area laced by creeks is one of the state's most beautiful parks. Sublimely sylvan, Beaver Creek State Park, near East Liverpool, surrounds the remains of the Sandy and Beaver Canal, which was built late in Ohio's short-lived canal era as a feeder to the Ohio and Erie Canal.

    Now a 3,038-acre preserve, the park includes lovely Little Beaver Creek, designated as a National Wild and Scenic River for its steep cliffs and thickly wooded bottomland. A pioneer village with a covered bridge and a reconstructed 1830 mill will appeal to history buffs. Hikers and canoeists will appreciate the rugged trails and scrappy river.

Don't miss the old locks, including Lusk Lock in an adjoining park on County 419. These locks are brick masterpieces that cost untold man-hours to build as part of a canal that was already obsolete by the time it opened.

Where: About eight miles northwest of East Liverpool off State 7.

Hours: The park office is open daily from 8:00 A.M. to 5:00 P.M.

Facilities: Creek fishing, hiking and bridle trails, primitive camping, horse camp, toilets and latrines, nearby golf course, picnic areas. The Sandy Beaver Trail, a twenty-one-mile path along the original canal route between East Liverpool and Elkton, also passes through the park.

For more information:

Beaver Creek State Park, 216-385-3091.

WEST BRANCH STATE PARK

The West Branch of the Mahoning River was dammed to form the 2,650-acre lake that is the jewel in the crown of this 5,362-acre state park. Come to picnic or camp, ride the trails, or buzz around M.J. Kirwan Lake at any speed you choose (except in no-wake zones). There's no horsepower limit, which makes it popular with water-skiers.

Nearby, soldiers mustered to march off to fight the War of 1812. Even before that, the spot was popular with westbound settlers, who learned from the Indians about a salt deposit where they could harvest this important food preservative.

Located between Akron and Youngstown, this park can be packed on peak summer days, but boaters can always find a quiet spot among the curving coves along the lake's shoreline. Horseback riders can roam twenty miles of leafy trails, and hikers can seek out the twelve-mile portion of the Buckeye Trail that winds through the park.

Where: North of exit 38 off I-76 east of Ravenna.
Facilities: Hiking trails, picnic tables with fire rings, bridle trails, group horse camp, boating, boat fuel and other marine supplies, food concessions, playground, boat ramp, cabins, fishing, sandy swimming beach with lifeguards and changing rooms, snowmobile trail, rest rooms, naturalist programs, camping, Rent-a-Camp (see page xx).
For more information:
West Branch State Park, 216-296-3239.

MOSQUITO LAKE STATE PARK

Despite its name, this state park near Warren is likely to be less buggy than many because the changing levels of the lake disrupt the life cycles of mosquitoes. The 7,850-acre Mosquito Creek Lake was dug in 1944 as part of a flood-control project. It's unusual because its waters flow in different directions at different times of the year. Most of the time, the overflow goes into the Mahoning River. When high levels are reached, however, the water spills over into the Grand River system and finds its way to Lake Erie.

The park can be crowded, but hiking paths lead off to a beaver pond, or you can wander the Mosquito Creek state wildlife area at the north end of the lake to watch for Canada geese, bald eagles, great blue herons, and white cattle egrets. During hunting season, the park is popular with duck hunters. The lake is very popular with fishermen, but no fishing is permitted in the wildlife area.

Where: On State 305 north of Warren.

Facilities: Sandy beach with changing booths; picnic tables with grills; playground; boat rental, fuel, and launch; fishing; ten-mile bridle trail; camping.

For more information:

Mosquito Lake State Park, 1439 State 305, Cortland, OH 44410. 216-637-2856.

5

Miami County Area

Just north of Dayton and west of Columbus, Miami County has more than its share of scenic, year-round canoeing attractions because of the Stillwater and the Great Miami rivers. The result is an abundance of green spaces where city dwellers can escape to hiking paths, canoe paths, and shaded picnic tables.

Four preserves form the corners of a square centered at Troy. You can explore them all in a weekend, allotting half a day each, or you can come here often and continue to make new discoveries in nature's ever-changing tapestry.

STILLWATER PRAIRIE RESERVE

A patch of rich, native prairie nestles at the curve of the Stillwater River in this 217-acre park. Turkey vultures and red-tailed hawks soar overhead, floating effortlessly on updrafts as deer browse in the woods. Preserved here are prairie plants such as shadbush, bluestem, columbine, and harebell. Thanks to a 1,600-foot boardwalk, you can tread lightly through tender marshes.

Part of the fun is that you have to wade the river to complete the trail.

The Hagan family came here from Pennsylvania in 1840. They built a water-powered sawmill, a road that today forms part of the trail, a home that can still be seen near the trail, and a log barn whose white pine planks were used in the park's rest rooms. The park, which follows the Stillwater River for a mile, is popular with cross-country skiers.

Where: One and a half miles west of State 48 on State 185.
Facilities: Rest rooms, picnic area, two fishing ponds.
For more information:
    Miami County Park District, 2535 East Ross Road, Tipp City, OH 45371. 513-667-1086.

GARBRY'S BIG WOODS SANCTUARY

In this 272-acre nugget of near-virgin forest, you'll see plants and animals that were abundant in Ohio before the settlers came. Many of them, including the undisturbed wet beech-maple forest, are now rare in the state. This is the largest stand of upland woodlands in Ohio, well worth a morning's stroll.

Great horned owls watch your progress through the forests of tulip trees, chinquapin oaks, and sugar maples. The trees shelter eastern wood pewees, deer, and white-breasted nuthatches and shade trilliums and large-flowered sessiles.

It's easy going for walkers or wheelchairs along a forty-two-inch-wide boardwalk about seven-tenths of a mile long. Stay on the path to protect fragile habitats and sensitive plants from intrusion. Come during the week in springtime, when the wildflowers are at their bawdiest, and you'll have this paradise almost all to yourself.

Where: Statler Road between Union-Shelby and Casstown-Sidney roads, south of US 36 and east of Piqua.
Facilities: Benches along the boardwalk. Picnic facilities and additional trails are planned.
For more information:
Miami County Park District, 2535 East Ross Road, Tipp City, OH 45371. 513-667-1086.

CHARLESTON FALLS PRESERVE

Most people come here to see the sparkling waterfall, but observers will find much more in the quiet valley that was carved over the centuries by the spring-fed Charleston River. Fossils found in the limestone date back 400 million years. Indian relics show that Native Americans were drawn to this site just as surely as are today's visitors.

Thanks to a rabbit warren of looping trails, you can walk for hours along the Redbud Valley, to the limestone cave, along the cliffs, past the pond, and to the waterfall. Look for uncommon plants such as wild columbine, walking fern, purple cliff brake, and rock honeysuckle. The fences are black locust, which was cut and split in these woods and installed by park staff.

The man-made pond is expected to be a marsh in the next century and a forest by the century after that. For now, however, it throbs with life—frogs and fish, wild ducks, buzzing insects, and bold raccoons.

Where: Ross Road, between State 202 and the Great Miami River.
Facilities: Small picnic area with drinking water. No fires are permitted, and there are no rest rooms.

For more information:
Miami County Park District, 2535 East Ross Road, Tipp City, OH 45371. 513-667-1086.

F. L. BLANKENSHIP RIVERSIDE SANCTUARY

Although it's only a five-acre patch of riverfront, this sanctuary is a good place to launch a canoe for further river exploration.

Where: One mile south of Covington on State 48 at Falknor Road.
For more information:
Miami County Park District, 2535 East Ross Road, Tipp City, OH 45371. 513-667-1086.

CEDAR BOG NATIONAL NATURAL LANDMARK

Just northeast of Miami County, Urbana in Champaign County has a wilderness area that is unique in Ohio. The only remaining alkaline bog in the state, supporting a stately stand of white cedar trees, Cedar Bog is a National Natural Landmark. Technically it's a fen, a spring-fed upwelling of water that consistently stays the same temperature and volume.

More than 100 species of birds and countless rare and endangered species, including the spotted turtle, live in this swamp along Cedar Creek, which soon joins the Mad River. The water supports a healthy school of brook trout, and the land under the boardwalk teems with life.

Where: South of Urbana off US 68.
Hours: Open for public tours only at 1:00 and 3:00 P.M.

Saturday and Sunday from April through September. The preserve is open Wednesday through Saturday, so call ahead for information.

Facilities: The mile-long boardwalk is wheelchair accessible; rest rooms are available.

For more information:

Cedar Bog National Natural Landmark, 513-484-3744.

Urbana Chamber of Commerce, 300 North Main Street, Urbana, OH 43078-1638. 513-653-5764.

GREATER DAYTON

Aullwood Center and Farm

At this working farm, programs are tied to the seasons. Come to see the projects in progress, the nature center and trails, and various exhibits.

Where: Ten miles northwest of Dayton at the junction of US 40 and State 48.

Admission: Yes.

Hours: Closed some holidays. Call ahead.

Facilities: Rest rooms, trails.

For more information:

Aullwood Center and Farm, 513-890-7360.

Convention and Visitors Bureau, Chamber Plaza, Fifth at Main Street, Dayton, OH 45402-2400. 513-226-8211.

Wegerzyn Horticultural Center

In a marshy setting on the Stillwater River, this center offers a formal rose garden, historical gardens, and beautiful bordered walkways.

Where: In Dayton, take I-75 to State 48, then turn left onto East Siebenthaler Avenue and look for the center on your left after the bridge.

Facilities: Gift shop, rest rooms.

For more information:

Wegerzyn Horticultural Center, 1301 East Siebenthaler Avenue, Dayton, OH 45414. 513-277-6545.

Cox Arboretum

This arboretum features an edible landscape, where fruits and vegetables form a lush garden. Nature trails lead through tall trees and among fifteen specialty gardens of wildflowers, shrubs, conifers, and other plants.

Where: Take I-75 south to the Miamisburg-Centerville Road exit. Turn left, then left again onto Springboro Pike.

Facilities: Rest rooms, gallery, visitors center, gift shop.

For more information:

Cox Arboretum, 6733 Springboro Pike, Dayton, OH 45449. 513-434-9005.

Inniwood Metro Gardens

This site covers ninety-two acres of gardens, pathways, and undisturbed natural areas. The herb and rose gardens are popular, and the park also has an impressive woodland rock garden.

Where: Take I-270 east to State 3, then go south to Dempsey Street, east to Spring Street, and north to Hempstead Road.

Facilities: Rest rooms.

For more information:

Inniwood Metro Gardens, 940 Hempstead Road, Westerville, OH 43081. 614-895-6216.

SYCAMORE STATE PARK

Not too many of the big, old sycamores are left, but they're being brought back in this new park, which only a few decades ago was mostly farmland. Today the 2,295-acre site is laced with hiking and bridle trails, many of them used in winter by snowmobiles.

Where: Just west of Dayton, off US 35.
Facilities: Fishing in small ponds, bridle trails, hiking trails, ice-skating, ice fishing, cross-country skiing, snowmobiling, picnic tables with grills, rest rooms, drinking water. Rangers are on duty, but the park office is not always open.
For more information:
   Sycamore State Park, 4675 North Diamond Mill Road, Trotwood, OH 45426. 513-854-4452.

6

Scioto River Valley

Sluicing through the heart of Ohio from Columbus south to the Ohio River, the Scioto River forms a 230-mile liquid highway that is roughly paralleled by a good motorway, US 23. Either route floats you away from city bustle into some of Ohio's most serene parklands and through millions of years of geological history.

Much of the natural history of Ohio was shaped by glaciers of unimaginable size and power. Written clearly on the face of the earth is the story of an enormous upheaval, slow and grinding, and mightier than most people can understand. A mile thick and many miles wide, great mountains of ice moved south millions of years ago, scouring away anything that got in their path.

Driving US 23 from Columbus to the Ohio River is a passage through some of Ohio's most interesting glacial history. Leaving Columbus, cross I-270 and note a series of kames (rhymes with names), conical hills that were formed by the Wisconsin glacier and its meltwater as it retreated northward. One of the most prominent, called Spangler Hill, is on the east side of the highway just north of Scioto Downs. Another prominent kame, on your left, is St. Joseph's Cemetery.

Starting at the rest area on the west side of the highway and paralleling the road as far as Circleville are long, linear ridges known as eskers—the most distinctive in the state. Their snaking pattern was sculpted by the north-south movement of the ice. The sandpit on the west side of the road just north of Circleville is an esker that has been mined of its sand and gravel.

South of Circleville, you pass through the Pickaway Plains, rich prairie land where the Shawnee Indians and their great chief Cornstalk roamed before the first white settlers arrived at the end of the eighteenth century. In 1774, Lord Dunmore's army of 3,000 men was sent from Virginia to attack the Shawnees. Outnumbered and outgunned, the Shawnees surrendered much of their land. Farmers moved in, and the modern agricultural era began.

Note the steep kames on the west side of the highway at Circleville. The highest, known as Black Mountain, was a Shawnee lookout. The small kame on the east just south of Emerson Road was the site of a burning stake where Shawnees are said to have killed their prisoners.

The area along the Pickaway-Ross county line is a boundary between two major physiographic provinces, the Central Lowland to the north and west and the Allegheny Plateau to the south and east. Note the prominent bedrock hills south of Delano Road on the east side of the highway. It's the Allegheny Escarpment and the beginning of the Great Plains, which end at the Rocky Mountains.

A mile south of US 23 and State 159, note the outcropping of shale and sandstone on the east side of the road. It was deposited during the early Mississippian period, about 345 million years ago, when Ohio was covered by a shallow sea.

East of the highway where the road crosses the Scioto River

just north of Chillicothe, you'll see Mount Logan, which is said to be the inspiration for the Great Seal of Ohio. On the west side south of Painted Creek is an outcropping of Ohio shale from the Devonian age 350 million years ago.

The road now leaves the river to travel through bedrock hills. It was at this point that the Illinoian glacier stopped. Visitors who explore the ridges find pieces of granite, a rock not native to Ohio, that were pushed here by the ice. To the east is Scioto Trail State Forest. Note a monument at its entrance honoring the "Scioto Hermit," William Hewitt. He lived in one of the rock caves in this area from 1820 to 1834. The rock you see is Berea sandstone, valued for its use in grindstones.

South of Piketon, the valley to the east of the highway is a broad plain that in ancient times was the course of the Teays River, which flowed from Virginia to Ohio and then west to the Mississippi. Its route was blocked by the first glacier and was so changed by succeeding glaciers that its bed is largely dry today except for Beaver Creek and parts of the Scioto River that use the old valley but flow in a different direction. The Teays Valley is clearly discernible on satellite photos, but highway travelers would never guess that a vast river system once covered the area.

About 1.8 miles south of Lucasville, on the east side of the highway where the river swings back close to the road, is an outcropping of about 300 feet of Early Mississippian age strata. The sandstone and shale are part of the Cuyahoga Formation deposited in the shallow sea millennia ago. Quarries in this area produce Buena Vista sandstone, which is used in building foundations and as laboratory countertops.

The finest paving brick in the nation was once produced here, using dark gray Portsmouth shale. The shale remains, but the industry no longer exists anywhere in Ohio.

Eastern bluebirds also nest in bluebird boxes

DELAWARE STATE PARK

On a reservoir formed by the Olentangy River, which joins the Scioto farther south, is a state park with many good features. Its best, though, is Bluebird Trail, where ninety nesting boxes that meet the rigid specifications required for mama bluebirds have been set among old farm fields that are gradually being reclaimed by the forest. The adjacent Delaware Wildlife Area expands the 1,815 land acres of this park. Boating and fishing are the chief interests here, and there is no horsepower limit. For this reason, nonfishermen may prefer to seek out campsites farther from the water. Hiking along the lake and through stands of young trees is placid and satisfying at any time of year.

Where: Off US 23, five miles north of Delaware.
Facilities: Fishing; swimming area; hiking trails; boat fuel, launch, and rental; campground with hookups; toilets; Rent-a-Camp (see page xx); naturalist programs in season; picnic area with rest rooms. In winter, sledding and ice-skating. Adjoins the Delaware Wildlife Area, with its many ponds and wildlife observation areas.
For more information:
   Delaware State Park, 5202 US 23 North, Delaware, OH 43015. 614-369-2761.

JANE DECKER ARBORETUM

Since 1863, loving hands have planted 116 species of trees on the campus of Ohio Wesleyan University in Delaware. Today the arboretum is not only an important teaching source but also an integral part of the university's landscaping.

   On a self-guided tour, you'll see species native to many areas of North America, as well as thirty-one from eastern Asia and twenty from Europe. One of the largest trees on campus is a Siberian elm. Carolina allspice spreads its distinctive, spicy aroma. The honey locus tree on campus is thought to have a macabre past. According to legend, a soldier fell on a thorn from one of the large honey locusts that once grew heavily in this area. The thorn pierced his brain and killed him.

Come in spring to see the snowy cover dropped by the cottonwood trees, in summer to see the yellow and white flowers of the Chinese scholartree, in fall to see whether the persimmons have fruited, and in winter to see the evergreens. Many of the trees are labeled; many are not.

Where: Ohio Wesleyan University is in Delaware. The tree tour area is bordered by Park, Sandusky, and William streets. It's best to call ahead for a map describing the tour and the trees.
For more information:
  Chamber of Commerce, 27 West Winter Street, Delaware, OH 43015. 614-369-6221.

COLUMBUS ZOO

Two tracts of land along the Scioto River were selected for a new state capitol in 1812, one for the capitol itself and the other for the state penitentiary. Today Columbus offers visitors some significant green spaces, including a zoological garden with elephants, giraffes, polar bears, kangaroos, gorillas, snakes and birds of all kinds, and thousands of plant species. The zoo is for all ages and is open every day of the year.

Where: Northwest of downtown. From I-27, follow the signs from exit 20, Sawmill Road.
Admission: Yes.
Facilities: Picnic area, rest rooms, children's zoo.

For more information:
Convention and Visitors Bureau, One Columbus Building, 10 West Broad Street, Columbus, OH 43215. 614-221-6623.

CHADWICK ARBORETUM

Established in 1980, the Chadwick Arboretum is a young and growing green space on the campus of Ohio State University in Columbus. Also outstanding is the Park of Roses, about five miles north of downtown in Whetstone Park. More than 10,000 roses in hundreds of varieties and colors make a fragrant setting for Sunday evening summer musicals and for strolling any day from the first rosebuds in May through frost.

Where: 2001 Fyffe Court, Columbus.
For more information:
Convention and Visitors Bureau, One Columbus Building, 10 West Broad Street, Columbus, OH 43215. 614-221-6623.

THE GARDENS AT GANTZ FARM

Grove City has been swallowed up by Columbus, but in 1830, when twenty-five-year-old Adam Gantz came here with his sixteen-year-old bride, Catherine, this was wilderness. Their 200 acres grew to 300 even before Grove City was laid out in the 1850s.

On the new part of the farm, a home was built from bricks baked on the site. Here Adam and Catherine produced fourteen children. Now a city park, the farm and restored farmhouse are used by schools as an education resource, but they're open to the public, too.

In the Garden of Yesterday, you'll see a kitchen garden typical of an Ohio farm in 1840. Herbs, fruits, and vegetables would have been planted, probably with a few frivolous flowers to feed the spirit. The Garden of Today is typical of herb gardens found in this century's dooryards: herbs planted for fragrance, others for culinary use, and still others for medicines. There's also a dye garden, a knot garden of low-growing plants that can withstand severe pruning and shaping, and a cutting garden that supplies the farm's education activities. The Garden of Tomorrow features herbs especially grown for landscaping purposes.

Where: From Columbus, take I-71 to I-270 west, then take the first exit and go south to the first intersection. Turn left onto Home Road and continue one mile to the park. From the south, take I-71 to Stringtown Road, go west about one-quarter mile, and turn right onto Gantz Road. Follow it to Gantz Road West, turn left, and continue on to the gardens.

Hours: Open daily sunrise to sunset, but best April through October.

Special note: Grove City has a folksy farmers' market every Saturday morning from mid-July to mid-September. For information, call 614-875-9762 and ask for directions and hours.

For more information:

The Gardens at Gantz Farm, P.O. Box 427, 2255 Gantz Road West, Grove City, OH 43123. 614-875-6300.

STAGE'S POND STATE NATURE PRESERVE

Swampy and teeming with life, this sixty-four-acre preserve is half shallow water and half land. It's nature's own monument to the great ice fields that scraped across this area 17,000 years ago, then receded to leave kettle lakes like this one. The preserve is at its most active during spring and fall waterfowl migrations, but the summer community includes nesting great blue herons and many other shorebirds.

In the open fields, you'll see quail and pheasant while hawks soar overhead and songbirds serenade. Oaks and giant hickory trees grow on higher ground, supplying fall color. Wildflower variety is best in springtime, but nature lovers can enjoy the drama here all year.

Where: Between Ashville and Circleville, just east of US 23 at Ward and Haggerty roads.
Facilities: Well water, nature trails, observation building, latrines.
For more information:
    Division of Natural Areas and Preserves, Building F, Fountain Square, Columbus, OH 43224. 614-265-6453.

SLATE RUN LIVING HISTORICAL FARM

Ponds and pastures, fields and meadows are operated here as they might have been 150 years ago. The farm's buildings, now restored, were built on this site between 1856 and 1881. Unhurried "farm folk" plant and harvest, cook and preserve in the old ways, using only the woodstove for heat and draft horses as tractors.

Where: South of I-270, take State 762 east off US 23. Then take State 674 south to Marcy Road.
Facilities: Picnic area, playground, water, rest rooms.
Hours: Closed Monday in the summer and Monday and Tuesday in the winter. Also closed Thanksgiving and Christmas. Otherwise, the farm is open daily, but hours vary seasonally so call ahead.

For more information:
Metropolitan Park District, 614-891-0700.

A.W. MARION STATE PARK

This 308-acre park near the glacial boundary encircles a 146-acre lake famed for its panfish, bass, muskellunge, and catfish. The 5-mile hiking trail follows the lake's shoreline, where on quiet mornings and at dusk you're likely to spot rabbits, pheasant, and deer in addition to the ever-present squirrels. Except for the four days in October when Circleville is invaded by half a million Pumpkin Festival revelers, this is a relatively forgotten park, overshadowed by the much larger and more glamorous Deer Creek State Park.

Where: From Columbus, take US 23 south to Circleville. Go east on US 22, then turn left onto Boulder-Pontius Road. The main park entrance is on Warner-Huffer Road. Follow the signs.
Facilities: Fishing (electric motors only), boat rental, launch ramp, hilly campground with sixty primitive sites and latrines, concession stand, rest rooms, two hiking trails through rolling woodland, picnic area with well water.
For more information:
   A.W. Marion State Park, 7317 Warner-Huffer Road, Circleville, OH 43113. 614-474-3386.

DEER CREEK STATE PARK

The Scioto River basin is Ohio's principal drainage system, a 50-by-135-mile watershed that drains 16 percent of the state's land area. Within its water resources program are four lakes on major Scioto tributaries: Delaware Lake on the Olentangy River,

Alum Creek Lake on Alum Creek, a tributary of Big Walnut Creek, Deer Creek Lake on Deer Creek, and Paint Creek Lake on Paint Creek.

Deer Creek State Park covers 6,348 acres and has a 1,277-acre lake. It's surrounded by another 3,710 acres of the Deer Creek Wildlife Area—so vast a preserve that, despite population pressure, it can still provide a back-to-nature vacation for those who seek out the path not taken, especially off-season and on weekdays. One of its drawing cards is a resort lodge that is a popular conference destination but is also a good place to dine on a night away from the campground.

Across the lake from the dam is an old lodge where Warren G. Harding's secretary of the interior is said to have hatched the Teapot Dome scandal. It is being restored for operation as a historical attraction. The Harding Cabin, not really the president's but built by Harding's attorney general, is a popular rental that sleeps nine. Put in a bid months in advance; rental is awarded by lottery.

Prehistoric Adena Indians are known to have roamed this area before modern Shawnee tribes moved in. Eventually, pioneer farmers cleared the oak forests. Deer fled, and hawks looked elsewhere for their prey. Now nature is reclaiming fields that not long ago were plowed and planted, and the deer, beavers, and other wildlife have returned in abundance.

Where: From Mount Sterling, go south on State 207, then east on Dawson-Yankeetown Road.
Facilities: Hiking trails, restaurant, bridle trails that serve as snowmobile trails in winter, lake with no horsepower limit, boat fuel, launch ramps, boat rental, marine store, lodge, cabins, full-facility campground, horse camp, sandy beach with lifeguard, nature center, amphitheater with nature programs. The resort has hotel-style accommodations, tennis, golf, a restaurant, and fitness facilities. For lodge and cabin reservations, call 800-282-7275.
Special note: Water levels in Deer Creek Lake are controlled by

the U.S. Army Corps of Engineers, so they can vary greatly. It can mean almost mosquito-free camping, but it also can mean that when water levels are at their lowest, navigation in the lake's shallowest portion is difficult to impossible. Know before you go.

For more information:

Deer Creek State Park, 20635 Waterloo Road, Mount Sterling, OH 43143. 614-869-3124.

TAR HOLLOW

The 16,126-acre Tar Hollow State Forest combines with Tar Hollow State Park to envelop travelers in a world of green. The forest is Ohio's third largest, and the state park is so rugged and heavily wooded that you can always find a secluded campsite along a sparkling stream or a deserted walking path in a moist and earthy hollow.

Where: Ten miles north of Londonderry off State 327.

Facilities: Bridle trails, fishing, swimming beach with lifeguards on peak days, hiking trails, picnic shelters, boating (electric motors only), boat launch, campground with showers and latrines. The Buckeye Trail goes through this area. A horse camp is located in the state forest.

For more information:

Tar Hollow, 614-887-4818.

Division of Forestry, Fountain Square, Columbus, OH 43224. 614-265-6694.

SEVEN CAVES

At Seven Caves, Paint Creek and Rocky Fork flow through what was once a giant ocean, forming a cluster of natural caves. It's a year-round destination, tempered in winter and cooler on hot summer days, where you can take a self-guided walk on challenging trails that wind up hills, down into gorges, and around rock formations.

Where: Fifteen miles east of Hillsboro on US 50, then south on Cave Road.
Hours: Every day.
Admission: Yes.
Facilities: Hiking paths, picnic area, snack bar, gift shop.
For more information:
      Seven Caves, 7660 Cave Road, Bainbridge, OH 45612-9501. 513-365-1283.

PAINT CREEK STATE PARK

The glaciers that sculpted this area left a playground of rocky hillsides, gorgeous gorges, and fish-filled creeks for Ohio visitors. The state park along Paint Creek, which empties into the Scioto River, offers 9,000 acres of land and 1,200 acres of water where you can boat and fish, photograph wildflowers, ride a horse, and enjoy see-forever views of the reservoir.

Where: Ten miles east of Hillsboro on US 50.
Facilities: Camping with electricity and dump station, eight miles of hiking trails, twenty-five-mile bridle trail, boating with unlimited horsepower, boat launch and fuel, showers, flush toilets, picnicking, camp store, pioneer village.
For more information:
      Paint Creek State Park, 7860 Upp Road, Bainbridge, OH 45612. 513-365-1401.

SCIOTO TRAIL STATE PARK

Jog off US 23 near Chillicothe, and you're suddenly in a green wilderness, seemingly miles from the rush and noise of the highway. It's a small green space, only 218 acres, with a couple of little lakes where swimming is not allowed, but it adjoins the almost 10,000 lushly wooded acres of the Scioto State Forest. Come for a picnic or to hide away for weeks in leafy hillsides that are alive with grouse, wild turkeys, and white-tailed deer.

Where: East of US 23 on State 372, then follow the signs.
Facilities: Picnicking, fishing (electric motors only), twelve miles of rugged hiking trails that follow the ridges, playground, camping, bridle trails through the adjacent state forest.
For more information:
   Scioto Trail State Park, 144 Lake Road, Chillicothe, OH 45601. 614-663-2125.

TULIPS IN PORTSMOUTH

It's a simple project that has grown to a mammoth size. Years ago, Arthur Koenig and his family planted a few tulips too early. A late snow snuffed out the tulip bed, but he noticed that one bloom had struggled through and stood alone, capped in snow. As the snow melted on the petals, it reminded Koenig of teardrops on a soft cheek, a sign that he should plant more. Today his beds of 150,000 tulips are one of Ohio's most glorious spring shows. Drive by anytime. Depending on the weather, tulips begin blooming in March and last through May.

Where: From US 23, take State 348 west to Henley-Comstock Road, then south to Diehlman Road, and watch for the signs.

For more information:
Portsmouth Convention and Visitors Bureau, Box 509, Portsmouth, OH 45662. 614-353-5824.

CANOEING THE SCIOTO BASIN

In addition to the Scioto River itself, year-round canoeing is possible on Deer Creek, much of Paint Creek, parts of Alum and Big Walnut creeks, and some of Salt Creek. Tributaries that can be canoed seasonally include parts of the Olentangy River and Big Walnut Creek, the Little Scioto River, Rocky Fork Creek, Scioto Brush Creek, and the upper reaches of Salt Creek. A brochure with maps, launch and access areas, hazards, and other information about boating this area is available from the Division of Watercraft. Request Section 3 (South Central).

For more information:
Division of Watercraft, 1952 Belcher Drive, Building C-2, Columbus, OH 43224-1386. 614-265-6480.

BIGELOW CEMETERY PRAIRIE

This half-acre state nature preserve of original prairie remains from the days when early settlers selected it as a cemetery. It's near Little Darby Creek, which lies west of the Scioto River, and is well worth a special trip.

Where: Eight miles west of Plain City on State 161, then a half mile south on Rosedale/Weaver Road. Continue west a few hundred feet on State 161 to see the covered bridge over Little Darby Creek.

For more information:
London Tourism Bureau, 66 West High Street, London, OH 43140-1075. 614-852-2250.

ALUM CREEK STATE PARK

Another of the waterways that eventually joins the Scioto River is Alum Creek, which was dammed in 1974 to create a 3,387-acre lake set in a 5,213-acre state park only minutes from downtown Columbus. Because it's so close to the city and has the longest beach this side of Lake Erie, the park can be packed on hot weekends, but its campsites are secluded, and its 9.5 miles of hiking trails are relatively remote. Even more remote are its 50 miles of bridle trails.

Plant life varies greatly, thanks in part to the glaciers, which left behind many different soils, seeds, and surfaces. Hike among beeches and maples, watching for the pink of spring beauties peeking up from under beds of fallen leaves.

Where: From US 23 between Delaware and Columbus, take Peachblow Road east to the park entrance.
Facilities: Camping, Rent-a-Camp (see page xx), picnic sites, hiking and bridle trails, boating with no horsepower limit, boat launch and fuel, full-facility campground, beach, concession stand, rest rooms.
For more information:
Alum Creek State Park, 3615 South Old State Road, Delaware, OH 43015. 614-548-4631.

SHAWNEE STATE PARK and STATE FOREST

The state park itself covers a stately 1,100 acres, but it's only a fraction of the enormous preserve that also includes the 59,603-acre Shawnee State Forest. It was all sacred hunting ground to Native Americans, a majestic forest that still inspires awe in those who explore its hazy and heavily wooded hills.

Although the total area of Wayne National Forest may be greater, this is Ohio's largest chunk of unbroken woodland—

breathtaking in its size, visual impact in all seasons, and ghostly, sacred silence. Live the good life in the resort lodge, cabins, or campgrounds with hookups, or head for the forty-three-mile backpacking trail through the state forest. This is a greenbelt for all persons in all seasons.

Where: Take US 52 west from US 23 at Portsmouth for seven miles, then follow State 125 seven miles northwest. The marina and golf course are off US 52, two miles west of State 125. To get to the park office, bypass the first entrance, which goes to the campground, and drive two miles more to the next entrance. The office is open weekdays from 8:00 A.M. to 5:00 P.M.

Facilities: In the state park are cabins, campgrounds, a resort lodge with an excellent restaurant, a golf course, boat rental, a landing strip, a boat launch, a marina, picnicking, swimming areas, and hiking trails. In the state forest are seventy-five miles of bridle trails and a horse camp, sixty miles of marked hiking trails (including parts of the Buckeye Trail), fishing lakes, and backpacking campsites. For campground information, call 614-858-4561. For lodge and cabin reservations, call 614-858-6621 or 800-282-7275.

Special note: More than 170 miles of roads lace the state park and state forest, offering green glades and stunning overlooks. Get maps at the park office.

For more information:

Shawnee State Park, Star Route, Box 68, Portsmouth, OH 45663-9703. 614-858-6652.

Shawnee State Park Lodge, P.O. Box 189, Friendship, OH 45630-0098.

Shawnee State Forest, Route 5, Box 151C, Portsmouth, OH 45662. 614-858-4201.

7

Hamilton County

Lucky the citizen of Cincinnati to live in a great city and yet be at the doorstep of equally great parks, forests, meadows, and waterways. City parks alone offer 44 miles of trails. Most of them are only half a mile to 1.5 miles long, but they loop and connect so you can ramble for miles. In larger parks, hikers can go from one trail to the next as long as their feet are willing.

Highlights of city parks include Bracken Woods, with its two-mile path through Buttercup Valley; the Wilson Wildflower Trail at Mount Airy; Burnet Woods, with its twenty species of native wildflowers under mature forests; and a trail at Stanbery Park that ends at a babbling creek spilling over limestone rocks. Follow it, if you like, all the way to the Little Miami River. Designed as a National Recreation Trail, it is not a loop, but it's worth backtracking for another view.

Also at Mount Airy is an ambitious ten-mile wilderness hiking trail through hardwoods and evergreens, including those in the arboretum.

Cincinnati's Ault Park winds through mature beech trees in a climax forest. The park is high over the Miami River valley, offering views of Mount Washington and the airport. In Caldwell Park, stroll a second-growth wood or amble under an arch of old beech trees.

All Hamilton County parks are open during daylight hours all year and are ranger patrolled twenty-four hours a day. A token admission is charged for motor vehicle entry. All have at least some facilities for people with physical impairments. Call ahead for hours at individual features of the parks and for information about outdoor education programs.

For more information:

Hamilton County Park District, 10245 Winton Road, Cincinnati, OH 45231. 513-521-7275.

Greater Cincinnati Convention and Visitors Bureau, 300 West Sixth Avenue, Cincinnati, OH 45202. 800-344-3445.

Cincinnati Park Board, 950 Eden Park Drive, Cincinnati, OH 45013.

EMBSHOFF WOODS AND NATURE PRESERVE

Because this 278-acre park is high above the Ohio Valley, it is a superior place to spot raptors soaring on the natural updrafts. Kestrels and many types of hawks are seen regularly; you may even see a bald eagle if you're lucky. Barred and great horned owls nest in the wooded valley. Except for the parcours fitness trail, the park is either heavily developed or in a completely natural state without designated hiking trails.

Where: From US 50, turn north onto Anderson Ferry Road, then east onto Delhi Pike or Mount Alverno Road. Follow either to Paul Road and the park entrance.
Facilities: Ice rink, athletic fields, golf course, picnic tables and shelters, amphitheater, fitness trail, rest rooms.

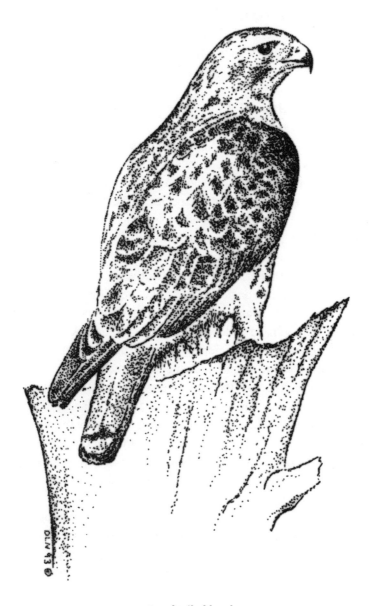

A red-tailed hawk

For more information:
Greater Cincinnati Convention and Visitors Bureau, 300 West Sixth Avenue, Cincinnati, OH 45202. 800-344-3445.

SHAWNEE LOOKOUT

There is much more to this 1,027-acre park than its superb hiking trails. One of its best-kept secrets is a scenic lookout over The Oxbow, an endangered wetland across the Great Miami River that harbors some of the rarest species in the state. You can get into the refuge only on organized expeditions through the Oxbow Society (2073 Harrison Avenue, Cincinnati, OH 45214; 513-521-7275), but the patient observer can spend hours at the lookout watching for tundra swans, double-crested cormorants, sandhill cranes, and bald eagles. Don't forget your binoculars.

Rarely seen inland, black scoters have wandered this far from the sea. So have willet and Eurasian wigeons. As more wetlands disappear under developments, these and other species will become even rarer, so take the time to see them here.

Because it's near the site where the Great Miami River flows into the Ohio, Shawnee Lookout has been a landmark for at least 14,000 years. Located on a 300-foot-high ridge overlooking the rivers, it was an obvious place for fortifications, from prehistory to modern times, and its variety of terrain ensured the Indians rich harvests of meat, fish, fruits, and nuts.

The first white settlers wrote about the Indian earthworks here in 1795, and by 1890 some professional archaeology had been done. The 1.4-mile Miami Fort Trail begins at the northeast corner of the ancient fort. A sign here shows the original map, dating to about 1817, which was made by early explorers of the site.

The stand of black walnut trees you'll pass is impressive

today, and archaeological digs have shown that the ancestors of these trees were vital to the Hopewell Indians. They ate the nuts and used the bark in their building projects. Another stand of exotic papaw trees bears a bananalike fruit that was also a food source for the Indians. The 300-year-old elm tree along the trail probably watched as Indian cultures gave way to white settlement. Massive trees like this were burned out to make canoes and cut down to lash together into rafts to run the river. The trees reseeded themselves and today form a rich stand of tulip poplar, oak, ash, and locust trees.

In springtime, you'll see Indian turnip, Dutchman's-breeches, squirrel corn, Solomon's seal, and Miami Mist, a waterleaf that is thought to grow only in the valleys of the Little Miami and Great Miami rivers. When warm weather comes, walnuts and acorns develop on the trees, while a cornucopia takes shape on wild grapevines and elderberry bushes. Clearly, the area was the Shawnees' supermarket as well as their lookout point.

Before or after the hike, visit the museum, where artifacts unearthed here are on display. It's open weekends from May through September. The collection includes arrowheads dating to the earliest occupation, as well as tools, grave goods, and pottery shards from cultures including the Fort Ancient and Hopewell Indians.

Little Turtle Trail is two miles long. Take your time. Because the trail is so varied, each habitat must reveal itself to you. It begins with an open field, where you may see a nesting bluebird or a white-tailed deer. Both, especially deer, are unusually abundant here. At the Crossroads (so called because the trail crosses itself), you may see snow fleas in winter and a wealth of insect life, including clouds of zebra swallowtails, in warm weather. Wildflowers bloom along the creek almost all year, starting with Dutchman's-breeches in spring, larkspur and fire pink in early summer, and white snakeroot and goldenrod in autumn. Even in the dead of winter, dried teasel seedpods and wind-dried goldenrod provide floral beauty.

This trail was named for Chief Little Turtle, a Miami Indian who was born in 1752. The burial mound dates to the Hopewell Indians (A.D. 200–450). As you complete the trail through young (sixty- to seventy-year-old) forest, watch for wild turkeys, rabbits, groundhogs, box turtles, and deer.

The park's third trail is named for Blue Jacket, the Shawnee chief whose real name was Marmaduke Van Swearingen. A white man, he was adopted by the Shawnees in 1771 and became a fearless warrior who fought against the settlers, captured Daniel Boone, and became a brigadier general in the British army at a time when the British were enlisting Indian aid against the upstart Americans. He died in 1810.

Although part of the trail is crisscrossed by power lines, the clearings made for the lines have become meadows that are alive with color. Look for jewelweed, thistle, pokeweed, and blackberry bushes, and watch out for poison ivy. Along the trail, wild sunflowers, blue lettuce, ironweed, wild carrot, and evening primroses bloom in summer, taking the place of spring flowers such as wild delphiniums and trilliums. Spend as much time as possible at the scenic overlook at the far end of the loop to gaze out over The Oxbow's teeming wetlands.

Where: Take US 50 west of Cincinnati to Mount Nebo Road, then turn right onto River Road, which becomes Lawrenceburg Road.

Facilities: Golf course, clubhouse with snack bar, picnic areas with tables and grills, launch ramp, rest rooms, museum, historical log cabin school. Parking for people with physical impairments is available at spots near individual points of interest.

For more information:

Hamilton County Park District, 10245 Winton Road, Cincinnati, OH 45231. 513-521-7275.

MIAMI WHITEWATER FOREST

This is a sprawling, 3,639-acre preserve of wetlands, brush, meadows, a lake, and both young- and old-growth forest. The 7.5-mile Shaker Trace is a hiking, equestrian, and biking trail, the longest in the county. Although the Shaker community inside the loop is not open to the public, it was occupied from 1824 to 1916 by the religious sect, which played an important role in Ohio agriculture. Members were required to be celibate, so as old Shakers died, there was no one to replace them. Their settlements throughout Ohio were gradually abandoned.

The other hiking trails are short but well laid out to show the best features of the terrain. The two-third-mile Tallgrass Prairie Trail gives hikers a glimpse of the original prairie, which park personnel are bringing back to life. With a hiker's rating of "Easy," the trail winds through the ecosystem that once covered a million square miles in America, including fifty-five of Ohio's counties. A French explorer describing the prairie in 1761 wrote of "immense meadows, interspersed with small copses of wood seemingly placed by hand. The grass is so very high that a man is lost among it."

Mowing, urbanization, draining of wetlands, and pesticides took their toll. Today true prairie is found only in scattered areas along old railbeds and forgotten fencerows, and sometimes in old cemeteries.

Prairie perennials have deep root systems that allow them to survive nature's ravages—prairie fires, drought, grazing. Their seeds have thick coats that can survive for years, if necessary, until the right conditions return for their germination. To reduce water loss during drought, some plants have thick leaves; others are thickly coated with a waxy substance that holds in moisture. Look for it in whorled rosinweed and compass plant. Blazing star and Virginia mountain mint have many fine, divided leaves— another way of reducing exposure to the moisture-sucking sun.

Many prairie plants are pollinated by wind, not insects, so

their colors can be drab. Those that do want to attract butterflies and bees are brightly colored. The result is a variety of inter-dependent growth, animals, birds, and insects.

Although no true prairie was found to exist in Hamilton County after the 1920s, park personnel have been working since 1980 to re-create 750 acres of prairie and 100 acres of wetlands, starting with the 5 acres you see on this hike. The young forest here has sprouted from seed since 1970, when mowing was dis-continued. Gradually, the big bluestem, Indian grass, and switch-grass are coming back, bursting into color in summer. Before they grow tall, there is time for pink shooting star, blue spider-wort, and golden alexanders to shine through. By late summer, they form a backdrop for tall wildflowers such as asters and tall coreopsis.

During this brief and easy hike, you'll see a fine stand of sassafras trees before entering a mature eastern deciduous forest filled with hardwoods: beech, sugar maple, ash, shagbark hick-ory, and oak trees. Leaving the forest, pause at the vernal pool to see if you can spot the salamanders that are breeding there. A vernal (springtime) pool fills with snowmelt and spring rains, supporting a unique ecosystem.

The 1.75-mile Badlands Trail winds through a moonscape of sinkholes, ravines, and odd-looking forms that wind and water have whittled from limestone. It's rugged going, rated "Chal-lenging." Stop often to listen for the pileated woodpeckers and watch for cottontail rabbits, skunks, chipmunks, chickadees, and towhees.

The three-quarter-mile Oakleaf Trail is shaded by stately old oak trees that are home to deer, raccoons, and mink.

Where: Near the Indiana border west of Cincinnati. Take I-74 to exit 3, Dry Ford Road. Follow this road north to West Road.
Facilities: Golf course, campground, visitors center, rest rooms, boat rental, tour boat, picnic areas, horse trails, and mile-long,

twenty-station parcours fitness trail. Five of the picnic areas can be reserved in advance.

For more information:

Hamilton County Park District, 10245 Winton Road, Cincinnati, OH 45231. 513-521-7275.

LAKE ISABELLA PARK

A tiny park along the Little Miami River, Lake Isabella packs a lot into seventy-seven green acres. There is the lake itself, which has been a fishing mecca since it was first stocked in the 1920s, as well as excellent bird watching because migratory waterfowl stop here in the spring and fall. Sit quietly in the wildlife blind and watch for kingfishers, green herons, bank swallows, mallard, and wood ducks, then stroll the woods to look for orange-and-black northern orioles and for prothonotary warblers, which nest in the elms and sycamores.

Where: Between Montgomery and Milford off I-275, and between Loveland and Madeira on Loveland-Madeira Road.
Facilities: Picnic facilities, both first-come and reservable, toilets, snack bar, playground, naturalist-led programs, canoe access to the Little Miami River, fishing and boating on Lake Isabella.

For more information:

Greater Cincinnati Convention and Visitors Bureau, 300 West Sixth Avenue, Cincinnati, OH 45202. 800-344-3445.

SHARON WOODS

Although this park is in a heavily populated area, its 737 acres have been parkland since 1932, so its natural beauty has been well preserved. Sharon Creek abounds in 450-million-year-old fossils that indicate this was once an inland sea. Glaciers gouged

A red fox

out lakes and ravines, setting the scene for today's waterfalls, gorges, and Sharon Lake. Geologists believe that a lake existed on this site 26,000 years ago.

The Gorge Trail takes you through 1.5 miles of geological history in about 45 minutes. It's rated "Moderate" because it's so hilly. A State Scenic Nature Preserve, the 20.86-acre gorge is a shutterbug's delight and a good place to watch for red foxes, white-tailed deer, and flying squirrels. Around the lake, you'll sight barn swallows, green herons, and wood ducks.

In winter, seek out the spot known as the 90-Foot Lookout. It's famous for its gigantic icicles. In summer, you'll have a better view of the wealth of fossils. Along the trail, you'll see beds of wild ginger, which Indians and pioneers used as seasoning. Watch out for the nettles and poison ivy.

Along the creek, note the sycamores. In early Ohio, giant sycamores grew hollow and were used as shelters or storage bins by Indians and early settlers. Your short walk will reward you with a long list of wildflower sightings: jack-in-the-pulpit, bell-wort, yarrow, henbane, wild comfrey, and woodland phlox, to name just a few.

Where: North of Cincinnati, just south of I-275, off US 42.
Facilities: Golf course, boating, picnic sites and reservable shelters, rest rooms, snack bar, bike trail, parcours fitness trail, playground, restored nineteenth-century village.
Special note: Operated by Historic Southwest Ohio, Sharon Woods Village is a typical nineteenth-century settlement comprising historic buildings moved here from other sites to save them from demolition. It's open May through October, Wednesday through Sunday. Admission is charged.
For more information:
Hamilton County Park District, 10245 Winton Road, Cincinnati, OH 45231. 513-521-7275.

WINTON WOODS

A graceland of green, this 2,375-acre park provides escape for the people of a thickly populated part of Greater Cincinnati. Although it's the most heavily used of the county's parks, it offers a few getaway areas where visitors can amble along the lake-shore, work out along a twenty-station parcours fitness trail, or hike.

The best walks are along the Kingfisher Trail, a mile-long path through the Greenbelt, a state nature preserve, and the Great Oaks Trail. Named for the 200-year-old oaks that are the grand-fathers among this forest of beech, oak, maple, tulip, poplar, sassafras, and hickory trees, the trail puts on a spring show of salt and pepper, wild delphiniums, and spring beauties, followed by a summer bloom of lobelias, trumpet honeysuckle, mayapple, and other wildflowers.

Where: North of Cincinnati, just south of I-275 between State 4 and US 127.
Facilities: Camping, boating, fishing, snack bar, visitors center, picnic areas and reservable shelters, rest rooms, hiking, biking, horse trails, playground, three ball fields, golf course.
For more information:
Greater Cincinnati Convention and Visitors Bureau, 300 West Sixth Street, Cincinnati, OH 45202. 800-344-3445.

WOODLAND MOUND

Paleo Indians settled this area along the Ohio River thousands of years ago. They were followed by the Archaic, Woodland, and Fort Ancient cultures. Modern tribes, including the Miami, Shawnee, Erie, Wyandot, and Delaware Indians, wandered through, hunting white-tailed deer and raccoons and harvesting nuts and berries.

The forest is in transition, gradually returning to nature after having been farmed. Some areas are maintained as meadows; others are planted with trees that will eventually grow thick and tall. The steep ravines and the river bluffs form the most dramatic scenery.

The hiking trails are short and easy, but they do have a story to tell. The Hedgeapple Trail is lined with Osage orange, and it winds around ponds that are abuzz with frogs, great-crested flycatchers, and dragonflies. In the Woodland Pond, see if you can spot a turtle or a freshwater snail. The Cattail Pond attracts red-winged blackbirds, which hide their nests among the plants.

The Seasongood Nature Trail meanders through an oak, maple, and redbud forest and across a creek. In the spring, bloodroot and dwarf larkspur peep through, followed by summer's show of sweet cicely, wild carrot, and jewelweed.

Where: Southeast of Cincinnati, south of State 125 (Beechmont Avenue), bounded by Old Kellogg Road, 8-Mile Road, and 9-Mile Road. Take exit 72 off US 52 and turn north.
Facilities: Parcours fitness trail, hiking trails, golf course and clubhouse, rest rooms, amphitheater, snack bar with dining patio overlooking the river, gift shop, nature center, ball fields, picnic areas with tables and grills, picnic shelters.

CINCINNATI ZOO AND BOTANICAL GARDEN

Because it's both a zoo and a botanical garden, this nature haven in the heart of Cincinnati merits more than one visit. Seasonal plantings light up all but the coldest days in the dead of winter. In spring, 250,000 bulbs burst into bloom just in time for the Spring

Floral Festival in late April or early May. Annual blooms are in full riot by June, when the public is introduced to zoo babies born the previous winter.

Walk through Jungle Trails, a two-acre rain forest habitat landscaped with tropical Asian and African plants and roamed by chimps, orangutans, and other small primates. In Wildlife Canyon, you'll find some of the zoo's rarest animals: Mhorr gazelles, which are extinct in the wild; little zebra duikers; elusive takins; and the highly endangered Sumatran rhino. The zoo's cheetah collection is one of the largest in the world.

The second oldest zoo in the nation, the Cincinnati Zoo houses one of the most diverse collections in the world—more than 750 species of animals, including 85 endangered species, and more than 3,000 kinds of plants. It's so old that three of its buildings are National Historic Landmarks—the Elephant House, Reptile House, and Passenger Pigeon Memorial. The last surviving passenger pigeon in the world died here in 1914.

Especially well-known for its breeding programs, the zoo has produced 37 lowland gorillas, half the world's total population of white Bengal tigers, and more black rhinoceroses (15) than any other zoo in the world. Its 108-acre Mast Farm in adjacent Clermont County is not open to the public, but it's an important part of the breeding and holding program. The Cincinnati Zoo also participates in The Wilds (see page 27).

The Butterly Aviary is alive with flight and flutter. It's said to be the most diverse insect collection in the nation. Polar bears cool off in their own icy pool. The zoo also has some Komodo dragons, the largest lizards in the world, and its aquarium is one of the largest inland aquariums in the nation.

Where: Take exit 5 (Dana Avenue) off I-71 or exit 6 (Mitchell Avenue) off I-75 and follow the signs to Dury Avenue and the main gate.

Hours: The Cincinnati Zoo is open every day at 9:00 A.M. Closing hours vary with the season.

Admission: Yes.

Facilities: Picnic area, restaurant, petting barn, rest rooms, stroller and wheelchair rental. All facilities are wheelchair accessible.

For more information:

Cincinnati Zoo and Botanical Garden, 3400 Vine Street, Cincinnati, OH 45200. 513-281-4700.

BICENTENNIAL COMMONS AT SAWYER POINT

If it were just another city park, Bicentennial Commons might not be mentioned in a book like this one, but its many features include a geological walk on which you can trace the Ohio River's time line back 450 million years. If you have trouble visualizing geological history, this stroll through the park will bring it into focus.

Old brick arches, once part of the L&N Railroad, mark an overlook with a good view of the riverfront and city skyline. The Riverwalk is a four-mile trail connecting the riverfronts of Cincinnati, Covington, and Newport. Don't miss the Flood Column, which shows where the Ohio River's great floods have reached in the past.

Where: Take the Pete Rose Way exit off I-75 or the Reading Road exit off I-71, then follow the signs.

Facilities: The park's open areas and amphitheater are popular settings for special events, so it can be crowded during such times. Up to 7,000 people can sit on the lawn during events at the Performance Pavilion. Other facilities include a picnic plaza, a fishing pier, tennis, ice-skating, roller-skating, volleyball, a

playground with a soft surface, a sculpture plaza, a fitness trail with sixteen stations, lawns for Frisbee play, and gardens.
For more information:
    Cincinnati Recreation Commission, 644 Linn Street, Cincinnati, OH 45203. 513-352-4000.

KROHN CONSERVATORY

Winter never comes to the tropical and desert gardens at Krohn Conservatory, where cacti and orchids, flowers and shrubs from all over the world spread a color spectacular every day of the year. More than 5,000 plants make up a wonderland of petals and plants, waterfalls and palms, not to mention a complete rain forest.
    The show begins in mid-January with cinerarias, cyclamens, and spring bulbs. By Easter the lilies, azaleas, hydrangeas, astilbes, and Clivias are in bloom, giving way on Mother's Day to an extravaganza of fuchsias, calla lilies, begonias, and Oriental lilies. Throughout the summer, the focus is on annuals, caladiums, and foliage plants. In autumn, the focus shifts to the chrysanthemum show, featuring gaudy Oriental varieties. The Christmas displays are breathtaking, starting with a giant tree made from potted poinsettias.

Where: Krohn Conservatory is in Eden Park. From I-75, take State 50. Turn right onto Martin Drive and then immediately onto the Newport Bridge. Turn right into Eden Park. From I-71 southbound, take the Reading Road exit. Turn left onto Elsinore, left onto Gilbert, and right into the park.
Hours: The conservatory is open every day from 10:00 A.M. to 5:00 P.M. On Easter Sunday, it opens at 7:00 A.M. and closes at 9:00 P.M. Christmas Day it is open from 10:00 A.M. to 9:00 P.M.

Admission: Donations are requested.

Facilities: Guided tours, rest rooms, gift shop selling Krohn-grown plants.

Special note: Eden Park, home of Krohn Conservatory, is one of Ohio's loveliest urban parks, offering stunning overlooks of the city and river, hiking trails (including a portion of the Buckeye Trail), a historic water tower, and a Moorish springhouse gazebo.

For more information:

Krohn Conservatory, Eden Park Drive, Cincinnati, OH 45202. 513-352-4090.

MOUNT AIRY FOREST AND ARBORETUM

Picture 800 acres of hardwoods and evergreens in a total forest of 1,450 acres smack-dab in one of Ohio's biggest cities. Because this was the first municipal reforestation project in the nation, it has had time to mature into a regal woodland. Native hardwoods shade what seems like miles of nature trails. Throughout the grounds, you'll find floral displays, garden after specialty garden, secluded picnic areas, and student and professional gardeners at work doing their research. Hauck Garden, located near one of the busiest intersections in the city, is a floral carnival of wildflowers, unusual trees and shrubs, and bright perennial borders.

Where: Eight miles northwest of downtown Cincinnati off I-75, on US 27 Colerain Avenue.

Facilities: Picnicking, trails, playground.

For more information:

Mount Airy Forest and Arboretum, 5080 Colerain Avenue, Cincinnati, OH 45202. 513-352-4080.

EAST FORK STATE PARK

Although it's next door to Hamilton County in Clermont County, East Fork State Park is claimed by Cincinnatians, who can lose themselves in its 8,420 land acres, 2,160 water acres, and 60 miles of hiking and horse trails. Some of the trails are part of the 1,200-mile Buckeye Trail, which encircles the state.

For serious backpackers, East Fork's Backcountry Trail is a bonanza. Register at the trailhead check-in station and check current water-level conditions. During heavy rains, when flood-gates are opened, the rivers may be impassable. Then make a two- or three-night adventure out of hiking the thirty-seven-mile trail through meadows and marshes, across rushing creeks, and into hilly forests and fragrant scrub. Follow the green blazes, which will lead you to two primitive campgrounds and one developed camp along the trail.

Gently rolling hills are covered with trees; plateaus sprout meadows carpeted with grasses and wildflowers. This is historic mill country, where gristmills and sawmills once sang along the East Fork of the Little Miami River. A church that dates to 1867, built on a site where Christians have worshiped since 1807, stands near the park office. Earlier still, pre-Columbian Indians hunted these hills and built a burial mound at what is now the south end of the park.

Nature watchers take to the trails to look for songbirds and raptors, chipmunks and the occasional deer, spring wildflowers and autumn color. Fishermen come in spring for fast-action fishing and in winter for ice fishing.

Where: Near the intersection of State 125 and State 222, twenty miles east of Cincinnati.
Facilities: Swimming beach with lifeguard on duty during the busiest days, campgrounds (including one for horses and riders),

rest rooms, picnicking, Rent-a-Camp (see page xx), rangers and campground hosts, hiking and bridle trails, beach concession, naturalist programs.

For more information:

East Fork State Park, P.O. Box 119, Bethel, OH 45106. 513-734-4323.

8

Lake Erie West

Lake Erie's shores are a beachfront playground for all Ohioans, but there is much more to this verdant coast. While the crowds are at the beach, steal away to quiet places like these.

CASTALIA QUARRY RESERVE

Some of Ohio's most beautiful green spaces began with what many today would call desecration. Topsoil was ripped away, and huge machines gored deep into the earth, cutting rock for building and for use as grindstones. Abandoned, many of these lands returned to nature. Pits filled with sweet water, and wildflowers and trees took root in canyon walls. Piles of crushed limestone became rock gardens, alive with wildflowers.

All 152 acres of this former quarry have been left au naturel since its last rocks were carted away in 1965. Climb its heights, and suddenly you're on top of the world, looking out over Sandusky Bay and Lake Erie. On a clear day, you can see the granite Perry's Victory and International Peace Memorial, far out in the lake.

Explore the land to discover glacial grooves and endangered plant species. In the rocks you'll see fossils that go back to the Devonian age, 400 million years ago.

Where: On both sides of State 101 one mile west of Castalia. Park in the lot on the north side of State 101 and cross to the trailhead on the south side of the road.
Facilities: None. Swimming, rock climbing, horseback riding, vehicles, and all activities except hiking are prohibited. Rock ledges are slippery and dangerous. Stay on the trails. Mountain bikes are allowed by permit only.
For more information:
Erie MetroParks, 3910 East Perkins Avenue, Huron, OH 44839. 419-625-7783.

WILLOW POINT WILDLIFE AREA

Willow Point Wildlife Area is a 645-acre wilderness used mostly by hunters and fishermen and has no facilities. Come at dawn and dusk to spy on the deer, muskrat, raccoons, mink, woodchucks, opossums, and waterfowl.

Where: Five miles northwest of Castalia off US 6, on Wahl Road.
For more information:
Willow Point Wildlife Area, 419-424-5000.

RESTHAVEN WILDLIFE AREA

Once a strip mine in what was originally a wet marl prairie, this terrain was left torn up and uneven when marl miners pulled out, but it is gradually regaining its original rough, robust prairie character. Called the Castalia Prairie by early settlers, it was once so thick that it was impenetrable. Now authentic prairie grasses such as big and little bluestem, Indian grass, and prairie dock can once again be found here.

The preserve's ponds, totaling 444 acres, support a cornucopia of bluegills, pike, bass, and bullheads. Cottontails, ring-necked pheasant, muskrat, and other forest friends scatter among the 1,828 acres of scrub and grass.

Where: South of US 6, bounded on the east by State 269, the west by Northwest Road, and the south by Vickery Road and State 101. Resthaven is six miles west of Sandusky and eight miles north of Clyde. Parking areas dot the preserve. For a map, stop at the headquarters, located on the south end of the wildlife area on Cement Road, Castalia.

Facilities: Boat launch.

Special note: Hunters use this area, so be aware of when hunting seasons are in effect.

For more information:

Resthaven Wildlife Area, 419-684-5049.

Department of Natural Resources, 925 Lima Avenue, Findlay, OH 45840. 419-424-5000.

PELTON PARK

Nature trails through sixteen acres of unspoiled oak forest put on a springtime show of meadow wildflowers and an extravaganza of autumn color.

Where: Pelton Park Drive off Hull Road, east of the Sandusky Mall.

Facilities: Picnicking, swimming pool, hiking paths, cross-country skiing.
For more information:
Erie MetroParks, 3910 East Perkins Avenue, Huron, OH 44839. 419-625-7783.

COUPLING RESERVE

Twenty acres of scented meadows, woods, and lowlands along the Huron River center on an old railroad station, where overnight bunking can be reserved by contacting the park office. Follow the nature trail any time of the year. In winter, sled or ski. Come in spring to enjoy the dogwoods. In summer, fish for white bass.

Where: State 13 and Hoover Road in Milan Township, adjacent to the Ohio Turnpike.
Facilities: Train car bunkhouses, meeting rooms in the historic station. Small, unpowered boats and canoes can be launched from May through October.
For more information:
Erie MetroParks, 3910 East Perkins Avenue, Huron, OH 44839. 419-625-7783.

OLD WOMAN'S CREEK STATE NATURE PRESERVE

The only national estuary on the Great Lakes, this 571-acre preserve is a teeming smorgasbord of bird, animal, and aquatic life. Technically, an estuary is a place where the land's fresh water meets the salty sea, forming a unique and separate waterway. Although salinity is not a factor here, the water is chemically different from that of Lake Erie and the rivers, and that makes for some of the most varied and exciting wildlife sightings in the state.

Elements that make up this transitional zone include the constantly changing barrier beach; rich plankton and schools of sunfish, shad, and perch; and upland forests of oak and hickory. You'll also find entire kingdoms of wildflowers—goldenrod, asters, milkweed, wild onion, spring beauties, mayapple, squawroot, and wild strawberries. The flowers attract insects and birds, which in turn attract the hawks and rodents that prey on them.

More than forty kinds of fish come here at some time during their life cycle. Many rare and endangered species of the plant, mammal, reptile, and amphibian kingdoms make their homes here. Tired birds stop to rest and feed during their migrations. More than 300 species have been recorded, including accidental visitors such as pelicans, a Louisiana heron, and wood storks.

The dedicated bird-watcher will want to come here often at different times of the day, season, and year. Pick up the bird checklist at the visitors center. It lists all the species that have been sighted. Ducks, herons, shorebirds, and songbirds are seen most of the year; others are seasonal.

Where: Off US 6 just east of Huron.
Hours: The hiking trail, observation deck, and beach access are open daily, 8:00 A.M. to 5:00 P.M. The visitors center is open Wednesday through Sunday, 1:00 to 5:00 P.M.
Facilities: Hiking trail, observation deck, beach access, visitors center.
For more information:
Old Woman's Creek Reserve, 2514 Cleveland Road East, Huron, OH 44839. 419-433-4601.

SHELDON MARSH STATE NATURE PRESERVE

Marshy and aflitter with juicy insects, this preserve is a paradise for birds and bird lovers. The same 300-species checklist used for Old Woman's Creek can be used for bird watching here.

Back in the 1950s, a doctor bought this land to create his own nature preserve, and he painstakingly peppered it with blue-bird nesting boxes. Today it's a nursery for families of eastern bluebirds, American kestrels, and, near the water, wood ducks and tree swallows. The work he began has expanded into a 330-acre preserve of barrier beach and marshes.

Snapping turtles up to thirty-five pounds may be spotted in the preserve. Watch for their heads, poking out as they glide almost invisibly through the water. The eastern box turtle that lives here has a yellow-and-brown pattern on its shell. The shy land turtle is seen after rains and in early morning or evening. The midland painted turtle, named for its "painted" red trim, is very common.

A painted turtle

The marsh has its snakes, of course, but they, too, have a place in nature's scheme. Don't mistake the eastern fox snake for a copperhead. It's a look-alike but is harmless and is found only in a few areas and in waning populations. You also may see other snakes, frogs and toads, and red-backed salamanders.

The marsh's botanical glory is its spectacular cardinal flower, a showy red spike that blooms in the woodland swamp. Some observers have called it America's most beautiful wildflower, and this is the place to see seas of it. From April through June, the preserve is a solid carpet of wildflowers that attract flocks of birds, especially wood warblers.

Where: East of Sandusky's Chaussee Road, off US 6. Look for the elaborate gates, which were originally the automobile entrance to Cedar Point Amusement Park. Abandoned because it was being eroded by the lake, the remains of the old road now form parts of the hiking path.

Facilities: None. Please stay on marked trails and do not picnic or swim.

For more information:

Division of Natural Areas and Preserves, Building F, Fountain Square, Columbus, OH 43224. 614-265-6453.

KELLEYS ISLAND STATE PARK

People find added romance and excitement in islands. So do birds and wildlife. Come here all year, not just for the beach and camping in summer but also for bicycling in spring and fall and for sledding and ice fishing in winter.

Gouged dramatically by the slow crawl of ancient glaciers, Kelleys Island is one of the best places in Ohio to view glacial scars in limestone bedrock. Although some of them were lost to quarrying, what remains is one of the largest and best collection of glacial grooves in North America.

The park can be crowded, and for good reason. Even on the hottest days, it's cooled by lake breezes. The beaches and campground, fossil hunting and fishing, bird watching and a carefree island lifestyle are strong drawing cards indeed. The island celebrates its monarch butterflies with a lively festival in September.

Where: Kelleys Island is reached by scheduled ferry or air service and by private boat or airplane. By ferry, you can take your car, camper, or bicycle. Or you can rent a bicycle or electric golf cart on the island.

Facilities: Camping (first come, first served; no reservations are available), picnic tables with grills, beach with changing rooms, rest rooms, five miles of hiking trails, boat ramp.

For more information:

Kelleys Island State Park, Kelley's Island, OH 43438. 419-797-4530.

CRANE CREEK STATE PARK

Turn-of-the-century shooters considered Lake Erie's marshes the best waterfowl hunting grounds in the nation, so wealthy sportsmen snapped up parcels of wetland to use as their own private hunting preserves. It may sound elitist, but at a time when other precious wetlands were being drained and industrialized, these sportsmen were saving a resource that we now know is a vital link in life cycles both ashore and deep in the lake.

Much of this marshland has been purchased by the state and is under professional wildlife management. One thing has not changed. For photographers and bird-watchers, this is still some of the best waterfowl hunting in the United States.

Although the park is named for the crane, the birds you see are egrets and herons. In fact, the largest heron rookery in the Great Lakes is offshore on West Sister Island. The only federal wilderness area in the state, it allows no visitors.

The state park covers only 79 acres, but the adjacent 1,821-acre Magee Marsh and the 6,000-acre Ottawa National Wildlife Refuge increase the wilderness impact of the park. Escape the beach crowds and find a quiet spot to watch for bald eagles, Canada geese, sandhill cranes, tundra swans, short-eared owls, and the dozens of other birds commonly seen here. Because this is where the Mississippi and Atlantic flyways cross, the bird watching is unparalleled.

Where: Seventeen miles east of I-280 on State 2. Or take exit 5 off the Ohio Turnpike. *Facilities:* Picnicking, fishing, swimming, lifeguard stations, hiking trails (including one that is wheelchair accessible), rest rooms. Nature programs are available through the Crane Creek Wildlife Experiment Station, 419-898-0960. Boats small enough to be carried to the beach can be launched here, but the park has no launch ramp. Magee Marsh has a bird trail, observation tower, and interpretive center.
For more information:
Crane Creek State Park, 13531 West State 2, Oak Harbor, OH 43449. 419-898-2495.

EAST HARBOR STATE PARK

The largest of Ohio's parks on Lake Erie, this sprawling park has a 7-mile band of brown-sugar beach stretching along an 1,152-acre preserve. The beaches are crowded on summer weekends, but the 7 miles of hiking trails provide escape into beach and marsh habitats where you can observe waterfowl, small game, Canada geese, and shorebirds.

Where: From Port Clinton, take State 163 west seven miles, then go north on State 269 for almost a mile.

Facilities: Camping with electric hookups, fishing, hunting, picnicking, swimming.

For more information:

East Harbor State Park, 1169 North Buck Road, Lakeside-Marblehead, OH 43440. 419-734-4424.

TOLEDO ZOO

Officials at the Toledo Zoo say that this is the only place in the world where you can watch hippos underwater. The African Savanna habitat and the koala collection are noteworthy, and the freshwater and seawater aquariums are among the largest in the country.

It takes more than one day to see all the zoo's plants, exhibits, animals, and attractions, spread among twelve buildings on thirty acres. In natural settings, you'll see giraffes, rhinos, elephants, lions, leopards, and many more animals. Zoo programs focus on the survival of endangered species such as gorillas, orangutans, cheetahs, and snow leopards.

The botanical gardens offer pleasant strolling, and the Spanish Colonial design of the buildings makes a good backdrop for photographs.

Where: Traveling north or south, take exit 201A off I-75 to State 25 south. Going east or west, take exit 4 off the Ohio Turnpike and follow Reynolds Road (US 20) north to Glendale Avenue.

Hours: Open every day except Thanksgiving, Christmas, and New Year's Day. Hours vary seasonally.

Admission: Yes. A parking fee also is charged.

Facilities: Rest rooms, food concessions, gift shop.

For more information:
Toledo Zoo, P.O. Box 4010, Toledo, OH 43609. 419-385-5721.

NORTH RIDGEVILLE'S GROWING ARTS

The truck farmer to much of America, northern Ohio is also the greenhouse capital of the nation. Now the hamlet of North Ridgeville in Lorain County has formalized the art of growing into an annual horticultural event in early May. In a self-guided, all-day Growing Arts tour, you'll visit about fifteen farms, strawberry fields, greenhouses filled with flowers, and garden centers. Write ahead to get a map.

Where: North Ridgeville is twenty miles west of Cleveland and can be reached via exits off I-90 or the Ohio Turnpike.
For more information:
Visitors Bureau, Box 172, North Ridgeville, OH 44039. 216-329-1881.

CATAWBA ISLAND STATE PARK

Perched on a peninsula that probes well out into Lake Erie, this park covers only eighteen acres, but it's also a staging area for South Bass and Kelleys islands. Come here to fish for record walleye, or to picnic while watching the foamy wakes of the enormous pleasure boat fleet that flits around the peninsula. Be forewarned: These fishermen are passionate about their sport. It's part of the fun, but it also can mean a tough time finding parking on weekends at the height of the fishing season.

Where: Take State 163 east from Port Clinton. Turn north onto

State 53, west onto West Catawba Road, and then left onto Moores Dock Road.

Facilities: Fishing pier, boat launch, ferry to South Bass Island, picnic tables with grills.

For more information:

Catawba Island State Park, 4049 East Moores Dock Road, Port Clinton, OH 43452. 419-797-4530.

SOUTH BASS ISLAND and OAK POINT STATE PARKS

It's only a short hop across the lake from Catawba Point, but South Bass is an island. Surrounded by blue water, this green space has an air of aloof and privileged escape.

It was near here during the War of 1812 that Oliver Hazard Perry's fleet bested the British once and for all. The majestic monument at the South Bass Island settlement of Put-in-Bay dominates the lake scenery for miles around.

Most visitors come for the fishing and quiet picnics, but the bird watching is good, and you can also see a small collection of glacial grooves. Lake views from the clifftops are spectacular.

Where: South Bass Island can be reached by passenger/car ferry, jet boat, or air. Bring your bicycle to explore the seventeen miles of roads on the island.

Facilities: Cabins (rented by lottery), fishing, picnicking, swimming, changing rooms, boat ramp, campground with showers and latrines. Oak Point State Park's chief function is to provide a one-acre corridor that allows visitors to get to the lakefront. It has docks and picnic tables.

For more information:

South Bass Island State Park, Put-in-Bay, OH 43456.

MAUMEE BAY STATE PARK

Maumee Bay State Park is found on Lake Erie near where it meets the Maumee River. Once a vast wetland where Indians harvested bountiful stores of wild rice, this 1,845-acre park was long ago drained and tamed, and its hardwoods were felled to make room for farm crops. Reforestation was begun only within recent decades.

The downside of all this newness is there are few old trees to nurture upland wildlife or to provide shade on sizzling days. On the plus side, the facilities in this park tend to be newer and more modern, and the marshy setting is a bird-watcher's dream.

The park, especially along the half-mile-long beach, is packed on summer days, but like almost all of Ohio's state parks, it offers quiet hideaways. The wildlife watching is exciting: beach birds, migrating hawks, meadlowlarks, short-eared owls, waterfowl of all kinds, shorebirds and bobolinks, and a growing population of woodland critters. At the nature center, you can aim remote cameras at wildlife in the marsh.

Where: From I-280, take State 2 (Navarre Avenue) east of Toledo. Go six miles east to Curtice Road, then continue north for three miles more.
Facilities: Hiking/jogging/biking trail, some shorter hiking trails (including a 1.9-mile boardwalk), lodge with full resort facilities (including an 18-hole golf course), marina, cabins, campground, Rent-a-Camp (see page xx), beach, nature center with naturalist, sledding, cross-country skiing. For campground information, call 419-836-8828. For cabin and lodge reservations, call 419-836-1466 or 800-282-7275.
For more information:
Maumee Bay State Park, 1400 Park Road One, Oregon, OH 43618. 419-836-7758.

SEAGATE AQUARIUM

Although larger and flashier aquariums can be found throughout the United States, and excellent freshwater and saltwater aquariums can be viewed at the Toledo Zoo, this little aquarium is a whale of a find for family travelers and for all "green" travelers who have a keen interest in underwater life. Found in the basement of the Society Bank and Trust, this free exhibit traces the entire span of fish life from the Maumee River to the Atlantic Ocean.

In the river tanks, you'll get close-up views of shiners, darters, all the popular Ohio sportfishing species (including bass, perch, walleye, and bluegill), and other fish, such as carp, that play supporting roles in the scheme of things. In the saltwater tanks are colorful displays of sea species such as grouper and royal gramma. Make sure to see the audiovisual presentation before touring the tanks.

Where: From the Ohio Turnpike, take exit 5 and go north to downtown exit 10, Summit Street. Turn south and watch for the bank on your left in about a mile. Metered parking spaces are available at the bank or next door at Portside Festival Market Place. If you'll be downtown for a longer period, use the parking garage across the street. Touring the aquarium should take no more than an hour.
Hours: Banking hours only.
Facilities: Rest rooms, shopping and dining in adjoining complex.
For more information:
Seagate Aquarium, 3 Seagate, Toledo, OH 43604. 419-259-8436.

JAMES H. MCBRIDE ARBORETUM

If you want to see the forests and prairies that greeted the first settlers in the Western Reserve, the Firelands campus of Bowling Green State University in Huron is the place to find them all in microcosm. Around the thirty-acre lakeside arboretum, you'll see patches of native tallgrass prairie, a bit of oak-hickory savanna, a mixed mesophytic forest, elm-ash and beech-maple forests, and a sampling of marsh wetlands dotted with native wetland wildflowers.

Called the Firelands because these were land grants to Connecticut farmers who were burned out of their homes during the Revolutionary War, this part of Ohio has a lot to offer the nature lover. Both the lake and the Huron River offer green spaces that are being brought back after years of commercial exploitation.

The arboretum is especially colorful in early May when the 150 flowering crab apple trees are at their pink-and-white peak, but the show goes on all year: evergreens in winter, flower-lined walkways in summer, delicate wildflowers in spring, and all the fireworks of an Ohio autumn. This is a young arboretum, first planted in 1991, but with the years its trees are maturing and its collections growing.

Where: The arboretum is at Firelands College on Rye Beach Road, half a mile south of State 2 in Huron.
Facilities: None, although rest rooms can be found in university buildings.
For more information:
James H. McBride Arboretum, Firelands College, 901 Rye Beach Road, Huron, OH 44839. 419-433-5560 or 800-322-4787, ext. 238.

MARBLEHEAD PENINSULA

Wind-swept Marblehead Peninsula juts out into Lake Erie forty miles east of Toledo and seventy miles west of Cleveland. It's a tourist mecca, filled with shops and art galleries, the largest U.S. Coast Guard station on the Great Lakes, restaurants, and a Chautauqua at Lakeside. Even if you are averse to crowds and "in" spots, come to see the delicate Lakeside daisies, which grow only here and in two spots in Canada. The little yellow wildflower is seen throughout the quarries that cover the entire inland portion of the peninsula.

Where: West of Sandusky, take the Bay Bridge (State 2) and turn right onto Bay Shore Road. Watch for the green-and-white signs that lead you through a circle tour of the peninsula.
Facilities: A permit is required to enter the Lakeside Daisy Preserve. Contact the Peninsular Chamber of Commerce well in advance.
For more information:
    Peninsular Chamber of Commerce, Box 268, Marblehead, OH 43440. 419-798-9777.

Sandusky Parks
Sandusky is famous for the profusion of flowers planted in its downtown parks. Take the free, self-guided walking tour. To get the brochure, call 800-255-ERIE.

TOLEDO'S PARKS

Like all Ohio's great cities, Toledo has hundreds of acres of green space where you can lose yourself in prairie and forest trails that are home to mink, muskrat, opossums, and deer. Contact the Metropark District for a map showing all the parks and their hiking trails, picnic areas, nature centers, and other features.

For more information:
    Metropark District, 5100 West Central Avenue, Toledo,
OH 43615. City parks, 419-472-6962. Metro parks, 419-535-
3050.

Wildwood Preserve Metropark
This park covers 460 acres and is centered by a grand, twenty-
two-room mansion that is open for tours. One hiking trail leads
through some of the last standing prairie in the state, with grasses
that tower overhead. Another winds through the cottonwoods
and sycamores that took root in the floodplain of the Ottawa
River. Still another explores soaring sand dunes pushed into
place by the punishing waves of the lake.

Where: West of downtown, east of I-75, at 5100 West Central
Avenue (State 120).
Hours: The park is open daily during daylight hours. The
Manor House is open Wednesday through Sunday, noon to
5:00 P.M.
Facilities: Picnic sites with grills, playground, rest rooms.
For more information:
    Wildwood Preserve Metropark, 419-535-3050.
    Greater Toledo Convention and Visitors Bureau, 401
Jefferson Avenue, Toledo, OH 43604. 419-321-6404 or 800-
243-4667.

Toledo Botanical Garden
The botanical garden is an outstanding sixty-acre center for the
art and science of horticulture. Of special interest are the shade
garden, medicinal and culinary herb gardens, roses, a fragrance
garden for people who are blind, antique vegetables and farm
crops, and a colorful perennial garden. All are tied together with
pretty paths, ponds, and gazebos.

Where: Six miles west of town off the West Central exit of I-475, at 5403 Elmer Drive; west of Reynolds Road and south of Central Avenue.
Admission: Free except during art festivals.
Facilities: Gift shop, art galleries, rest rooms.
For more information:
    Toledo Botanical Garden, 5403 Elmer Drive, Toledo, OH 43615. 419-536-8365.

Oak Openings Preserve

This 3,674-acre greenbelt is popular with cross-country skiers in winter and joggers and bicyclists in summer. It's threaded with trails and brooks and adjoins patches of a state forest preserve.

Where: South of US 20 between State 64 and Berkey Southern Road.
Facilities: Designated ski trail, bicycle and fitness paths, bridle trails, picnicking, playground, ice-skating, fishing, walking center.

9

Lake Erie East

MENTOR MARSH

Pick a still summer day to steal away here for pensive nature observations of this 644-acre wetland that is alive with bird and insect life. During spring and fall bird migrations, bird-watching action is hot and heavy. Even in winter, you'll spot mallard, gulls, rock doves, and perhaps a few lonely loons, grebes, or hawks.

Where: West of Painesville, 3.5 miles on State 283, then half a mile north on Corduroy Road.
Facilities: Observation tower, hiking trails, 1,850-foot wheel-chair-accessible boardwalk. No rest rooms or drinking water.
For more information:
    Mentor Marsh, 216-265-6453.

HEADLANDS DUNES

Made up of a 16-acre state nature preserve and the 125-acre

Headlands Beach State Park, all of it adjacent to Mentor Marsh, this area includes an incredible sugar-sand beach that rivals anything the Caribbean has to offer. The downside is that the parking lot, which holds almost 4,000 cars, sometimes has to be closed because it is full.

Still, there are always ways to leave the madding crowd and strike off on your own. The bird watching here is unequaled, so you may want to spend most of your time in the nature preserve, trudging the sands and training binoculars on faraway sites. The Buckeye Trail touches this area, but following it will quickly lead you out of the preserve.

Where: Headlands Beach State Park is north of I-90 on State 44. The state nature preserve is at the east end of the state park.
Facilities: Concession stand, hiking trails (mostly in adjacent preserves), rest rooms, drinking water, picnic tables with grills, fishing pond, swimming, lifeguard.
For more information:
Headlands Beach State Park, 9601 Headlands Road, Mentor, OH 44060. 216-257-1330.

HACH-OTIS STATE NATURE PRESERVE

You'll find no facilities here, just the reedy silence of an eighty-one-acre nature preserve along the Chagrin River. Bank swallows and kingfishers nest in the clay banks along the river, and dozens of other species make their home in the tall maples and oaks. Stroll the area anytime to watch for deer and foxes, woodpeckers and barred owls. In springtime, many people make an annual pilgrimage to see the spectacle of wildflowers.

Only about a mile to the south, the Buckeye Trail threads through the river basin, skirting another wildlife area, the 1,912-acre North Chagrin Reservation on SOM Center Road.

Kingfishers on the lookout for fish

Stop at the nature center for information and maps describing self-guided walks along ten miles of trails. You'll spot pintail, mallard, and more of the Canada geese that have made such a brave comeback in Ohio, as well as deer and small game. Rangers at North Chagrin can also provide information about Hach-Otis.

Where: Hach-Otis State Nature Preserve is one mile east of Willoughby Hills, off US 6. Go 200 yards north on State 174, then east on Skyline Drive to the dead end.
For more information:
      North Chagrin Reservation, 216-351-6300.

NELSON LEDGES

Satiny green stone, stark gray cliffs, silvery slivers of falling water, and rocks that have been worn into a sculpture garden form a small but very exciting park. Entire mansions are formed by, under, and among the huge rocks, which have names such as Old Maid's Kitchen and Devil's Icebox. Hiking trails put you through a real workout, making you squirm through tight squeezes, climb and fanny-sled, crawl and stretch.

Now part of the 167-acre Nelson-Kennedy Ledges State Park, the ledges have been an Ohio landmark since time began. Only Nelson Ledges are open to the public at this time

Where: South of US 422 and east of Hiram on State 282.
Facilities: Picnic tables, grills, toilets, drinking water, short but challenging self-guided trails. No ranger is on duty, but information is available from Punderson State Park, where permits must be obtained before venturing into Kennedy Ledges.
For more information:
Punderson State Park, 216-564-2279.

PYMATUNING STATE PARK

Sprawling, 14,650-acre Pymatuning Lake is more in Pennsylvania than Ohio, but this state park in Ashtabula County is all Ohio's. It's a heaven-sent green space and an alternative to the crowded Lake Erie shores. Pymatuning, "place where the man with a crooked mouth lives," was one of the Indians' favored hunting spots. Marshy and still, it bounded with small game, birds, and big game such as bears and wolves.

Then came the white settlers, who drained the swamps, dammed the rivers, cut the trees, and began farming. During the Great Depression, hard times for farmers, the state began buying up the lake's shoreline to save it for recreation purposes. Today the park totals 3,500 acres.

Where: Forty miles north of Youngstown, east of US 6. State 85

crosses the lake at its midpoint. Turning north or south at the causeway will take you to park access points, but campers should turn south to reach the campground office.

Facilities: Many good developed and undeveloped campsites, fishing, swimming beaches, picnic tables with grills, hiking trails, lodges, boat ramps and fuel, snack bar, playgrounds, naturalist programs, ice fishing, iceboating.

For more information:

    Pymatuning State Park, Andover, OH 44003. 216-293-6329.

GENEVA STATE PARK

We have friends who have circumnavigated the globe in their sailboat. When talk turns to mean seas, they rank Lake Erie right up with the Indian Ocean, the North Sea, and the Gulf Stream. The lake is shallow, which means that sudden winds can whip it into a frenzy very quickly. Geneva State Park, which lies just to the west of the razzmatazz resort village of Geneva-on-the-Lake, can take a pounding from the lake, but it's a great place to watch boats running before the storm. And when the lake is still, it serves up awesome sunsets and sunrises.

    The biggest drawing card, of course, is the broad, brown-sugar beach, but it's also interesting to walk the inland areas to watch for birds and catalog the unusual wildflowers.

Where: Just west of Geneva-on-the-Lake. Take Lake Road West off State 534.

Facilities: Beach with lifeguards, fishing, boat launch, campground with hookups and flush toilets, cabins, picnic tables with grills, changing booth.

For more information:

    Geneva State Park, P.O. Box 429, Geneva, OH 44041. 216-466-8400.

10

Cuyahoga River Valley

Native Americans called the river Kah-ih-og-ha, meaning "crooked." From the time the first canoes plied its waters and the first deerskin moccasins crept along its banks, the Cuyahoga River was central Ohio's most important highway, landmark, and boundary. It was a no-man's-land, so important to travel and trade that no tribe claimed it as its own.

Glaciers gouged out its first channel, which was sculpted and worn by restless waters until it formed endless esses, twisting its way through a corridor that would join two great cities, Cleveland and Akron. The Cuyahoga, which was known to some of America's earliest explorers, is shown on seventeenth-century maps of the New World. Moravian settlers came in 1786 and built a settlement where Tinkers Creek meets the river.

By 1827, the Cuyahoga was providing water to the Ohio and Erie Canal, which replaced the fractious river as a main transportation artery between Cleveland and points south. The city of Akron rose as a result of the canal. By the time the Ohio and Erie was replaced by the railroad, both Cleveland and Akron were thriving industrial cities.

CUYAHOGA VALLEY NATIONAL RECREATION AREA

The national recreation area surrounding the Cuyahoga River covers 32,000 acres, an area so large that it offers everything from symphony concerts to the silence of a wintry woods, from screaming toboggan runs to timid trilliums along a deserted footpath.

One of the best ways to get an overview of the park is aboard the Cuyahoga Valley Railroad. Aboard this historic train, you'll ride along the river, often seeing wildlife and wilderness areas that aren't accessible by road. Several itineraries and boardings are offered, including a Nature Train with National Park Service rangers on board. Twice a month, the train goes slowly through the valley while rangers point out nature and wildlife.

The Buckeye Trail, which runs the entire length of the state, also runs the length of the park. Countless hiking, biking, and bridle trails lace the park, many of them suitable for cross-country skiing in winter.

The recreation area also is crisscrossed by roads and highways, including some of northern Ohio's busiest arteries. Get a map first, then determine where you want to enter and explore.

For more information:

Cuyahoga Valley National Recreation Area, 15610 Vaughn Road, Brecksville, OH 44141. 216-526-5256 or 800-433-1986.

Ohio and Erie Canal District, Pinery Narrows, and Metropark Bedford

Within this area, you'll find the Canal Visitor Center, where rangers can direct you to the activities that interest you most. The old Locktender's House served the Twelve-Mile Lock. Later it was used as a blacksmith's shop, hotel, saloon, and grocery store. Now it's being turned into a museum that will tell the fascinating story of the canal.

In Metropark Bedford, you'll find the Gorge Parkway through Tinkers Creek Gorge, a steep-walled slit that is 140 to 190 feet deep. A National Natural Landmark, it spills over with unusual species of ferns, mosses, lichens, and liverworts, and in the spring, it offers a dazzling wildflower display. Within this part of the park are hiking and ski trails, a driving range, and hills that are open for sledding in winter.

Opened in the autumn of 1993 is a 20-mile towpath trail of crushed limestone that leads walkers and bicyclists along the old canal route from Rockside Road, past State 82, across Boston Mills Road, across State 303, and on to Bath Road in Akron. In a $1.8 million project, workers filled in fallen riverbanks, tunneled under a railroad track, built an 88-foot bridge at Peninsula, and constructed a 1,674-foot boardwalk through an ecologically sensitive wetland called Stumpy Basin.

For more information:
Cuyahoga Valley National Recreation Area, 15610 Vaughn Road, Brecksville, OH 44141. 216-526-5256 or 800-433-1986.

Hinckley Reservation
Part of the Cleveland Metroparks System, this 2,288-acre park at the southern end of the Cuyahoga Valley National Recreation Area is best loved locally for its 90-acre lake and craggy, 250-million-year-old ledges. Laced with springs that feed the lush vegetation clinging to the sides, Whipps Ledges are as high as 350 feet above the lake in places. Another series of ledges, Worden's Ledges, was decorated in the 1940s with carvings.

Hinckley's claim to national fame is its turkey buzzards, which return from the south each year in mid-March to nest in the trees among the cliffs and canyons. Their unbroken 150-year record is followed by the press as closely as the swallows' return to Capistrano.

Where: From Cleveland, take I-271 southwest to State 303, then turn west onto State Road, following the signs to Hinckley Lake.
Facilities: Hiking trails, baseball diamond, boat launch, bridle trail and stables, sledding and skiing, food concession, rest rooms, picnic shelters. Rangers are on duty at all times at 216-243-7860, where emergencies can be reported. For information about the Cuyahoga Valley Railroad, call 216-657-2000 or 800-468-4070.
For more information:
    Metroparks, 4101 Fulton Parkway, Cleveland, OH 44144. 216-351-6300.

Hale Farm

A working farm and bustling village, Hale Farm operates as it would have 150 years ago, growing and harvesting, preserving and spinning, sugaring in winter, selling land, conducting weddings, making soap, and so on. Built around an actual farm, the village also contains reconstructed buildings that were moved here to save them from demolition. Many special events are held throughout the year, providing a glimpse of farm life in early Ohio.

Where: Hale Farm is east of I-77 between Everett Road and Ira Road. Take the Wheatley Road exit off I-77, then go south on Revere Road to Everett Road. Hale Farm can also be reached via the Cuyahoga Valley Railroad (800-468-4070).
Hours: Open daily, 10:00 A.M. to 5:00 P.M. from mid-May through October; limited hours the rest of the year and some holidays depending on special events. Call ahead.
Facilities: Restaurant, gift shop, rest rooms, picnic settings, walking trails.
For more information:
    Hale Farm, 2686 Oak Hill Road, Bath, OH 44210. 216-666-3711.

BLOSSOM MUSIC CENTER

One of the nation's premier orchestras makes its summer home at one of the most beautiful natural settings in the music world. Adjoining the Cuyahoga Valley National Recreation Center, the Blossom Music Center rambles over 800 acres of rolling hills and grassy lawns.

The summer home of the Cleveland Orchestra, Blossom also hosts a summer-long season of rock, jazz, country, and classical concerts in the open air. Bring a blanket or lawn chair, or sit theater style under the pavilion. Either way, the acoustics are incredibly good.

One of the favorite summer evening gathering spots for music lovers throughout northern Ohio, Blossom offers three dining alternatives. Bring your own picnic to enjoy at tables throughout the grounds or on the patch of hillside you've chosen for attending the concert. Have dinner catered at Blossom Grove, a party center that accommodates groups of 25 to 500. Or make reservations at the comfortable outdoor Blossom Restaurant, where a varied menu offers everything from salads to steaks and seafood, all prepared with a Continental flair.

Where: Twenty-eight miles southeast of Cleveland in Cuyahoga Falls. From Akron, take State 8 north, then turn west onto Steels Corners Road. From the Ohio Turnpike, take exit 11 or 12.

Admission: Yes.

Facilities: Amphitheater, picnic tables and grills, restaurant, rest rooms, tram service from the parking lot to park points of interest.

For more information:

Blossom Music Center, 1145 West Steels Corners Road, Cuyahoga Falls, OH 44222. 216-566-8184 (Cleveland) or 216-920-8040 (Akron).

THE GARDEN CENTER OF GREATER CLEVELAND

So beautiful are the grounds of the Garden Center and all of University Circle that wedding parties by the dozen come here on sunny days for photo sessions. Compact but colorful and varied, the center has an herb garden, a rose garden, a wildflower section, a lily pool, and a Japanese garden. The reading library is extensive and offers a good place to spend winter days planning spring planting while gazing out over snow-covered grounds.

Where: East of downtown, off Euclid Avenue, in University Circle (off Wade Oval between the Museum of Art and the Museum of Natural History).
Hours: The Garden Center is open Monday through Friday, 9:00 A.M. to 5:00 P.M.; Saturday, noon to 5:00 P.M.; Sunday, 1:00 to 5:00 P.M. The gardens are open all year, dawn to dusk. The library is closed Monday.
Facilities: Parking garage, shop, library. For horticultural information, call 216-721-0400.
For more information:
     The Garden Center of Greater Cleveland, 11030 East Boulevard, Cleveland, OH 44106. 216-721-1600.

LAKE VIEW CEMETERY

Beautiful grounds and gardens, stately trees, and monuments to leaders such as President James A. Garfield and oil magnate John D. Rockefeller sprawl over 285 manicured acres. Drive or stroll the grounds for a deep sense of Cleveland social and natural history. Especially poignant is a monument to children and teachers who died in a school fire in 1908.

Where: 12316 Euclid Avenue at East 123rd Street.

Hours: Open daily, closing at 5:00 P.M. in the summer and 4:00 P.M. in the winter.

Facilities: None.

For more information:

Lake View Cemetery, 12316 Euclid Avenue, Cleveland, OH 44106. 216-421-2665.

THE BUCKEYE TRAIL

The 1,200-mile Buckeye Trail, which encircles the state, goes through the Cuyahoga Valley. Blue blazes lead you through the two sections that are within the Cuyahoga Valley National Recreation Area. They're considered strenuous hikes, with some steep hills, and can be muddy after rain.

The 5.6-mile Columbia Run section starts at the Jaite Trailhead, goes through a field on a power line access road, and continues into a young mixed maple-oak forest to an old carriage road lined with majestic oaks. From the heights, watch for hawks soaring effortlessly on thermal drafts and view the valley's changing seasonal clothing.

In the open, sunny areas, you'll see thistles, milkweed, and daisies spreading their wares for goldfinches, butterflies, and bees. You'll enter a forest of tall oaks, with an underforest of maples. From the ridge, you'll descend into a moist, cool ravine with mature beeches and maples. Listen for black-capped chickadees as you cross the creek and climb out of the ravine through old farm fields and across busy Columbia Road.

If you have time, take the side trail to Blue Hen Falls, then return to the Buckeye Trail, cross Boston Mills Road, and follow the trail through woods that parallel I-271 into an open field and past the caretaker's home on National Guard property. Follow an old roadbed downhill, across a creek, up a ridge, and then down a steep hill into the village of Boston.

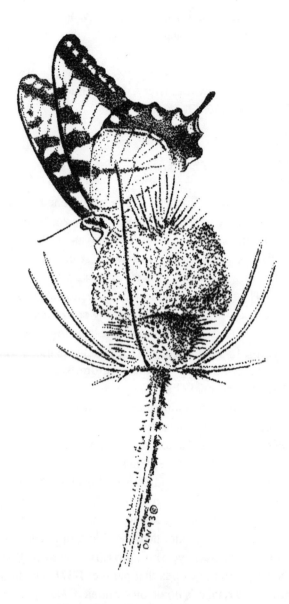

A tiger swallowtail on a teasel

The four-mile Boston Run section of the trail goes south on an old paved road, then away from the river and into a grassy area and a young oak-hickory wood. The remains of an old apple orchard give way to older beech and maple trees. Stay with the blue blazes, watching for darting wildlife as you cross Boston Mills Road. You'll follow a wooded ravine, cross over the Ohio Turnpike, and emerge in a grove of white pines.

Slow your pace if possible as the trail guides you through mature oaks, then fields, and past a borrow pit and small pond. The plant life is unusual, and there is a good chance you'll see deer and a variety of birds. The trail follows Akron-Peninsula Road for a short distance, turns into a pine forest, and descends into a cool valley cut by Boston Run. The valley is a wildflower garden filled with ferns and flowers. The trail then climbs out of the creek valley to reach the Pine Lane Trailhead, where another section of trail begins.

Where: The Jaite Trailhead is on Vaugh Road, east of Riverview. The Boston Trailhead is at Boston Mills Road and Hines Hill, Boston. The Pine Lane Trailhead is north of State 303 east of Peninsula.

Special note: It is not recommended that you tackle the Buckeye Trail without information and maps from the Buckeye Trail Association. Adult membership is $15.00 per year, students $7.50.

For more information:

Buckeye Trail Association, Box 254, Worthington, OH 43085.

Brandywine

Once an entire village, this community had already dwindled to only four houses and a school by 1900. It never recovered and, except for one home, was bulldozed to make room for the interstate. However, the old Lemoin House, built in 1859, remains part of the Cuyahoga Valley National Recreation Area. The

81-acre site has observation decks with a dazzling view of the 120-foot-deep gorge and the rushing, 63-foot waterfall that so long ago brought the wheels of industry to this valley.

Where: Take the Brandywine Road exit off I-271 and follow the signs to the gate.
Facilities: Picnic area, boardwalk, biking and hiking trails, overlook, rest rooms. The Inn at Brandywine is a bed and breakfast in a Greek Revival mansion built in 1848. For information, call 216-467-1812. Carriage Trade is a livery service offering horse-drawn carriage or sleigh trips, gourmet picnics, and tours. For information, call 216-467-9000 (Cleveland) or 216-650-6262 (Akron).

METROPARKS ZOO

One of the oldest zoos in the United States, Cleveland's Metroparks Zoo has more than 3,000 animals on its 165 acres. Ramble for hours, observing big cats, primates, birds, rhinos, seals, and all things great and small.

The zoo's most impressive feature is its new (1992) Rainforest, which is home to 600 animals belonging to 118 species and covers 2 acres on two levels. You're greeted by a 25-foot waterfall that cascades down what appears to be the ruins of an ancient temple. Chattering tropical birds, bursts of mist, and the heavy fragrance of rich, damp earth re-create a tropical rain forest faithfully.

Following the trail from one level to another, you'll circle a giant kapok tree and see butterflies flying free. Then climb the circular staircase inside the tree to an observation deck. A scientist's hut, much like one you might see in the rain forest, has been re-created. Animals and reptiles, from the Madagascar hissing cockroach to the Bornean orangutan, complete the scene as you make your way to a torrential rainstorm that repeats every fifteen minutes to the delight of the jungle amphibians that live inside.

Where: Take the Fulton Parkway or West Twenty-fifth Street exit south off I-71 and enter the zoo from the Fulton Parkway or the Brookside Park entrance.

Hours: The zoo and Rainforest are open all year except Christmas and New Year's Day. Hours vary seasonally.

Admission: Admission is charged to the zoo and the Rainforest. Admission to the Rainforest only is available. Tickets are available at the entrance or through Ticketmaster, 216-241-5555. Zoo admission is free to residents of Cuyahoga County and Hinckley Township in Medina County.

Facilities: Restaurant, rest rooms, gift shop, programs. Zoo administrators can be reached at 216-661-6500.

Special note: Strollers aren't permitted in the Rainforest. If you have a backpack for the baby, it will come in handy here.

For more information:

Metroparks Zoo, 3900 Brookside Park Drive, Cleveland, OH 44109. 216-661-7511.

CLEVELAND MUSEUM OF NATURAL HISTORY

On the first rainy day of your green tour of Ohio, rush to the Museum of Natural History in Cleveland's University Circle and dazzle the children with some of the biggest and best dinosaur exhibits in the nation. Robotic dinosaurs have become all the rage, which makes these stark, supersize skeletons even more impressive.

Among the most important exhibits are the head of a 20-foot-long armored fish that swam the seas of Cleveland 360 million years ago, the only mounted example of a 70-foot-long *Haplocanthosaurus delfsi* (plant-eating dinosaur), and the only known specimen of a *Nanotyrannus* skull.

The museum also has displays devoted to all the earth sciences, including a planetarium show and an outdoor garden with live native species such as bald eagles, hawks, deer, and owls. The museum's gardens include a sample of a northern hardwood forest, floodplain plants, a fern garden, a prairie, an Allegheny nonforested opening, a mixed mesophytic forest, a bog, and a Buckeye section of the Mississippi Basin.

Where: East of downtown, off Euclid Avenue, at University Circle.
Hours: Monday through Saturday, 10:00 A.M. to 5:00 P.M.; Sunday, 1:00 to 5:30 P.M.; open until 10:00 P.M. Wednesday from September through May. Closed major holidays.
Admission: Yes.
Facilities: Gift shop, rest rooms, wheelchair access throughout.
For more information:
Cleveland Museum of Natural History, 1 Wade Oval Drive, Cleveland, OH 44106. 216-231600.

AKRON ZOOLOGICAL PARK

The Akron Zoological Park is the kind of place to return to time and again to make friends with the animals and picnic under the shade trees. The zoo is small, with only 200 animals, but it's user-friendly. Children can feed cows, goats, lambs, and chickens, then see exotic monkeys and big cats and walk into an aviary to get a close view of macaws and bald eagles. Of special interest is an underwater viewing area where you can observe busy river otters.

Where: Take the Copley Road exit off I-77 and go east to Edgewood Avenue.

Hours: Monday through Saturday, 10:00 A.M. to 5:00 P.M.; Sunday and holidays, 10:00 A.M. to 6:00 P.M. Evening hours June through August. Closed mid-October to mid-April, but visit the park during the holidays to see the lights and at Halloween for the Zoo Boo.

Admission: Yes.

Facilities: Concession stand, gift shop, free parking, picnic areas, stroller rental.

For more information:

Akron Zoological Park, 500 Edgewood Avenue, Akron, OH 44307. 216-434-9567.

STAN HYWET HALL AND GARDENS

Warren Manning, one of the fathers of American landscape design, created these gardens in the 1920s for rubber baron F. A. Seiberling, and it's the only one of his landscapes in the United States that has survived intact. The gardens are magnificent, with walkways and allées, seas of roses and beds of annuals, spectacular views of the Cuyahoga Valley, stands of trees, a greenhouse, and a tropical conservatory. The show from early May to early November is spellbinding, but the gardens are beguiling even on winter days when the crowds are gone, bare trees stand stark against the blue sky, and the evergreens are crowned with snow.

The sixty-five-room mansion, dark and woody in Tudor Revival fashion, is open for tours.

Where: Take State 18 west of downtown to Portage Path. Go 1.5 miles north on Portage Path.

Hours: Closed Monday and major holidays. Hours vary seasonally, so call ahead.
Admission: Yes.
Facilities: Gift shop, snacks.
For more information:
   Stan Hywet Hall and Gardens, 714 North Portage Path, Akron, OH 44308. 216-836-5533.

F. A. SEIBERLING NATUREALM

Named for the B.F. Goodrich rubber magnate who contributed so much to the saving of green spaces as Akron grew, the 100-acre Naturealm is part of a 400-acre park system. Sixteen acres form an arboretum grouped according to growth habit: upright, weeping, pyramidal, and so on. Paved, graded walkways make the scenic path accessible to everyone, and it ends in an observation deck where visitors can relax and watch for birds. The flowering crab apples in May are a special drawing card.

   The rock and herb garden near the parking lot is a good place to see glacial rocks, as well as seventy-five species of medicinal, aromatic, and culinary herbs. The boardwalk crosses a pretty pond, where you may see a turtle or hear a frog croaking at the chuckling waterfall. In a demonstration lot, prairie grasses have been planted to show what the Ohio prairie looked like before the sodbusters arrived.

   In the earth-sheltered visitors center, look out over the landscape to view birds and animals, peer into a bee hive, interpret a weather station, play some electronic nature games, and see marsh and woodland exhibits. Programs are excellent and frequent, and naturalists are on hand to answer your questions.

Where: From I-77 take the State 18 exit (Akron-Medina Road) and go east. The road becomes Smith Road. The visitors center

is on Smith Road between Sand Run Road and Riverview Road.
Hours: The visitors center is open every day except Christmas,
Thanksgiving, and New Year's, from 10:00 A.M. to 5:00 P.M.
The park is open daily from 8:00 A.M. to sunset.
Facilities: Hiking trails, drinking water, toilets, gift shop, natu-
ralist, special programs.
For more information:

F. A. Seiberling Naturealm, 216-836-2185.

Metro Parks of Summit County, 975 Treaty Line Road,
Akron, OH 44313. 216-867-5511.

QUAIL HOLLOW STATE PARK

Conrad Brumbaugh was in tall timber when he first began
exploring this area around 1810. The huckleberry thickets were
so dense that folks sometimes got lost while picking the succulent
blue berries. Most of the Delaware Indians were gone by then,
forced westward. Brumbaugh hunted deer, pigeons, and wild
turkeys in the swamps and thick forests around Congress Lake,
built a log cabin, and battled rattlesnakes and bears as he wrested
a working farm out of the wilderness.

The wind-worn headstones of the Brumbaugh family
cemetery can still be seen in this 698-acre state park. Although
it's small, the park offers 12 miles of hiking trails and 4 miles of
bridle trails through habitat that could be, except for the loss of
giant elm trees, much like the land that was so bountiful with
fish, fowl, and game when Brumbaugh first arrived.

The original homes burned, but the rambling forty-room
mansion built by the land's second owners, the Stewart family,
is now the Natural History Study Center. It's a working study
center and is not furnished in period pieces, but do take a look
at the painting over the mantel. It shows the entire original
Stewart estate.

This young screech owl freezes in position, hoping you'll miss him

Workshops and nature hikes are held at Quail Hollow all year. They center on the original Stewart family herb gardens, which have been restored, the beaver pond, a bird blind located in the peat bog, and other intriguing habitats.

Where: Southeast of Akron, off I-77. Take exit 120, go southeast on State 619 to Hartville, and then go north on Congress Lake Road.

Hours: The Natural History Study Center is open weekdays from 8:00 A.M. to 5:00 P.M. In winter, cross-country ski equipment is available for rent at the study center Monday through Saturday, 9:00 A.M. to 5:00 P.M.; Sunday, noon to 5:00 P.M.

Facilities: Picnic tables with grills, historic sites, rest rooms, water, fishing in Congress Lake Outlet (but not the beaver pond), hiking trails (including a half-mile paved trail for all users, including the physically impaired).

Special note: If you don't have insect repellent with you, stick to the hiking trails that are south and east of the study center.

For more information:

Quail Hollow State Park, 13340 Congress Lake Avenue, Hartville, OH 44632. 216-877-6652.

SEA WORLD OF OHIO

Just east of the Cuyahoga Valley in Aurora, Sea World of Ohio is the only aquatic park of its type in the Midwest. It's the home of Shamu the killer whale, as well as oceans of seals, dolphins, otters, and other sea creatures. The Penguin Encounter is hilarious entertainment and offers a rare chance to see penguins posing and diving, strutting and preening in a cold, natural habitat. Sea World is entertaining, but it's also a serious scientific settlement where studies continue and injured sea creatures are treated and rehabilitated.

Where: Two miles northwest of Aurora, just east of I-480 and north of the Ohio Turnpike.

Admission: Admission fees are high, but they include all entertainment, exhibits, professional waterskiing and boat shows, and much more.

Facilities: Gift shops, restaurants, wheelchair and stroller rental, playground.

For more information:

Sea World of Ohio, 1100 Sea World Drive, Aurora, OH 44202. 800-63-SHAMU.

TINKERS CREEK STATE PARK

Although it's one of the smaller state parks and is in an area of high population density, the 740 acres of Tinkers Creek State Park are a green refuge from the interstates and crowded communities of northern Ohio. It's marshy, which makes for interesting nature watching. Walk the 3.5 miles of trails on a quiet weekday, and watch for beavers and muskrat. In springtime, the bird show is superb, especially among waterfowl. A good population of Ohio songbirds stay the season.

Where: North of exit 13 off the Ohio Turnpike.

Facilities: Swimming beach, hiking trails, picnic shelters, rest rooms, changing rooms.

For more information:

West Branch State Park, 5708 Esworthy Road, Route 5, Ravenna, OH 44266-9659. 216-296-3239.

GARDEN OF ROSES OF LEGEND AND ROMANCE

You are promised a rose garden and one of the best arboretums in the Midwest when you visit Ohio State University's Agricultural Research and Development Center at Wooster. Established in 1882, the center works with field crops, livestock, orchards, flowers, and trees.

The eye-popping array of roses is tightly laid out in a formal garden crisscrossed by what seems like miles of pathways. Called by the Greek poet Sappho the "Queen of Flowers," the rose has remained a favorite for centuries. The focus in this garden is on sustaining old varieties, with all their legend and romance.

The moss rose, which was cultivated in the south of France in the seventeenth century, grows here in varieties from throughout the ages. The Species roses shown here include the Austrian Copper, which was known before 1597. It's thought that the Alba rose cultivated here was brought to England by the Romans before A.D. 100. Gallicas have been used medicinally and commercially since the twelfth century.

This is a garden for flower lovers, but also for those who love art and literature, because the roses are grown and shown in their historic and literary context. Most exciting of all is to know that these ancient varieties are being tended and saved.

Where: In Wooster, follow the signs on US 250 to the Ohio Agricultural Research and Development Center.
For more information:
Garden of Roses of Legend and Romance, 1680 Madison Avenue, Wooster, OH 44691. 216-263-3700.

SECREST ARBORETUM

Considered unique by many plant enthusiasts, this 85-acre treasury of trees has more than 2,000 species and varieties of trees and shrubs. Flowering trees have been planted to bloom through the seasons. The rhododendron garden, with 135 selections that burst into May bloom, is especially popular with visitors. Crab apple, azalea, and holly species also provide a color spectacle, while sections of hardwoods serve as a living laboratory for university students and scientists. The *Taxus* collection, with more than 100 selections, is the largest in the United States.

Blooms appear in April, and autumn color lasts through October, but with its large collections of evergreens, the arboretum is a popular destination in winter, too.

Where: In Wooster, follow the signs on US 250 to the Ohio Agricultural Research and Development Center.
For more information:
Secrest Arboretum, 1680 Madison Avenue, Wooster, OH 44691. 216-263-3761.

11

Maumee River Valley

THE MAUMEE RIVER

When the first white settlers came to Ohio, they found great
forests, streaming rivers, and fertile prairies teeming with life
and promise. Those who faced only the normal hardships of
pioneer life were the lucky ones. The unfortunate bumbled into
a vast wasteland that for centuries had been shunned and feared
by Indians.

The Black Swamp covered about 2,000 square miles in
northwestern Ohio. Roughly the size of Connecticut, it was
about 120 miles long and an average of 40 miles wide, a swath of
hardwood forest so dense that sun couldn't pry through to dry the
dank wetlands. The waters were stinking and sulfurous; wolves
roamed the woods. Mosquitoes and poisonous snakes were an
ever-present danger.

Today all that terror has been tamed into farmland and recreation areas. The Maumee River is a State Scenic and Recreation

River flowing through portions of five counties between Toledo and the Indiana border.

The river, which was the only highway early people had through the area, is still a major greenbelt serving hikers and boaters and offering roadside parks and vistas to the highway traveler. The Maumee is canoeable all year, except for the rapids between Waterville and Perrysburg. They can range from Class 1 to Class 3, depending on water levels, and should be approached with current local advice.

The scenic portion of the Maumee starts at the state line and continues for forty-three miles through a forested floodplain past sharply rising valley walls to the US 24 bridge west of Defiance. The recreation section starts at the US 24 bridge and covers fifty-three miles to the US 20–State 25 bridge at Perrysburg. In this section, the channel widens and valley walls are less steep.

The valley saw many skirmishes during the French and Indian War and the War of 1812. Two canal systems, the Miami and Erie and the Wabash and Erie, burrowed through during the canal era, and the river basin was changed further as the Black Swamp drainage program progressed.

Where: More than thirty recreation areas, historic sites, and access points are found along the Maumee River between Toledo and Antwerp.

Facilities: Canoeing, historic sites, fishing, hiking trails, tennis, swimming pools, boat launch, playgrounds, field sports. For a list of the specific sites and their facilities, contact the Division of Natural Areas and Preserves. Request "Boating on Ohio's Streams, Section 1" (Northwest).

Special note: Take special precautions when boating or canoeing the Maumee. Its immense power can be unleashed unexpectedly by sudden rains or when log jams occur. Note, too, that many tracts of land along the river are private. Don't put ashore except at designated recreation sites.

Canoe the Maumee River

For more information:
Division of Natural Areas and Preserves, Building F, Fountain Square, Columbus, OH 43224. 614-265-6453.

GOLL WOODS

One place where you can get the full impact of the Black Swamp is at Goll Woods in Archbold, where a 321-acre reserve of virgin forests has the moist, dark look of the ancient forests that met the first white settlers to come to northwestern Ohio. Wildflowers are varied and abundant in the earthy, aromatic woods. On the prowl are foxes, white-tailed deer, spotted salamanders, and turtles. Wide-eyed owls observe the whole show.

Where: Take State 66 2.2 miles north from Archbold. Turn west onto County Road F, then south onto Goll Road (County 26).
Facilities: Six-mile hiking trail, observation area, rest rooms.
For more information:
Goll Woods, 419-265-6453.

Ohio Department of Natural Resources, 1889 Fountain Square Court, Building F-1, Columbus, OH 43224.

MAUMEE STATE FOREST

Under timber management in this state forest are 3,068 acres of woodlands that are accessible only by fifteen miles of bridle trails and five miles of trails for all-terrain vehicles (ATVs).

Where: About three miles south of Swanton, turn east onto Archbold Lutz Road.
Facilities: Bridle trails, ATV trails, Windbreak Arboretum in the ATV trail section.
For more information:
Maumee State Forest, 1-3357-D, Swanton, OH 43558. 419-822-3052.

MARY JANE THURSTON STATE PARK

Lucky the Maumee traveler to have both the lakefront state park and this one along the river itself. Its sister park, Providence Metropark on the other side of the river, adds to the overall size of this 555-acre park. Primarily a picnic stop for tourists who come to this area for its many historic sites, the park is a serene spot to watch the river and its passing parade of boats, water-fowl, and anglers.

The hiking trails are short but have a lot of impact. One

THE TIFFIN RIVER
The Tiffin River, which runs into the Maumee from the north, and the Auglaize, which joins it from the south, are also canoeable for miles. A new hiking trail, the Northwest Ohio Rivers Council Memorial Trail, roughly follows the Tiffin River, starting at Evansport on the Defiance-Williams county line. It's designed in loops of six and seven miles but at press time was too new for much information to be available. *For more information:* Defiance Area Tourism and Visitors Bureau, Box 7010, Defiance, OH 43512.

---

follows the old canal towpath into the time-warp village of Grand Rapids; another winds inland into the woods.

Where: Twenty miles southwest of Toledo, off State 65.
Facilities: Primitive camping, some sites with electricity, picnicking, lake and pond fishing, boat launch, marina, sledding, concession stand, latrines, flush toilets.
For more information:
　　Mary Jane Thurston State Park, 1-466 State 65, McClure, OH 43534. 419-832-7662.

HARRISON LAKE STATE PARK

Ohio's northwesternmost state park at Harrison Lake is as quiet as the lakefront parks are busy, although it can sometimes be crowded with shunpikers from both Ohio and nearby Michigan. It's one of the smaller state parks, only 142 land acres and 107 water acres. Only electric motors are permitted on the lake, adding to the quiet atmosphere.

　　Harrison Lake was created when the Black Swamp was drained—not much of a beginning for a lake that is now sweet and still. It has a pleasant little beach and some of the best night catfish fishing in the area. The lake is rimmed with a walking trail.

Where: South of US 20, between US 127 and State 66.
Hours: The park office, found east of County 27 on the north side of the lake, is open weekdays from 8:00 A.M. to 5:00 P.M.
Facilities: Fishing, swimming, picnicking, hiking trails, launch ramp, hilly campground with hookups and showers, Rent-a-Camp (see page xx), some campsites for people who are handicapped.
For more information:

Harrison Lake State Park, Fayette, OH 43521. 419-237-2593.

12

Muskingum River Valley

The largest river lying completely within Ohio, the Muskingum had a natural role in transporting Indians, the first missionaries, and the earliest settlers. The first permanent settlement in Ohio was founded at Marietta, where the Muskingum and the Little Muskingum meet the Ohio River, in 1788. By 1841, a series of locks and dams made the river navigable as far north as Dresden, where trading vessels could enter the Ohio and Erie Canal for access to Lake Erie.

For 112 majestic miles, the Muskingum River flows from city to city through floodplains forested with walnut, elm, cottonwood, and soaring sycamore trees. Along the banks, thickets of papaw ripen their sweet fruit in the fall to the delight of hungry birds.

The muskellunge fishing has declined in recent decades, but the river remains a lush source of shovelhead catfish, three species of black bass, and walleye. Also found in the river are rarer species, such as sand darters, northern madtoms, mooneyes, and channel darters.

Although there are many ways to explore the green valley and the river itself, all paths lead to Muskingum River State Park.

MUSKINGUM RIVER STATE PARK

Most other Ohio state parks center on a scrap of Lake Erie shoreline, a reservoir, or a forest. Muskingum River State Park is narrow as a sliver, but it follows the magnificent Muskingum River from its source at the confluence of the Walhonding and Tuscarawas rivers at Coshocton to Marietta, where it flows into the Ohio.

More a parkway than a park, it is reached by various roads. The best way, of course, is to travel by water. Locking through is part of the fun, and one of the campgrounds is accessible only by boat. This is, however, a big river that calls for substantial boating savvy and skills. If you do try it in a small boat, be aware that other, larger boats can present a more serious hazard than the river itself. No horsepower limits apply. Canoeists may prefer to portage at the locks.

Pontoon boats, canoes, rowboats, and powerboats take to the river with houseboats and motor yachts. Public and private launch ramps are available throughout the route. Get current state-of-the-river information before launching, and take special care on the upper channel between Dresden and Ellis. It's unmarked and not easy to follow.

By car, your destinations will be the old lock sites where the picnic and camping areas are located.

Where: From Coshocton to Marietta. The park map outlines the routes available and shows the locations of facilities. The park's main office is at Lock 10 in Zanesville.

Facilities: All lock sites have picnic tables, grills, and latrines. Drinking water is available at all of them except Lock 9 at Philo. Public launch ramps are found at Locks 4, 5, 6, and 11. Fee ramps are located near Locks 2, 7, and 10. A twenty-two-site camping area is available at Lock 11, off State 60 and County 49. Primitive campsites, which can be reached only by boat, are found at Lake Chute, Lock 5. Fishing is permitted from boats and lock sites but not from lock walls. An eighteen-station fitness trail follows the river for half a mile from the Y-bridge in Zanesville to the park office.

For more information:

Ohio Division of Tourism, Muskingum River Parkway, P.O. Box 2806, Zanesville, OH 43701; 614-452-3820. Or call 800-BUCKEYE.

Marietta Tourist and Convention Bureau, 316 Third Street, Marietta, OH 45750. 614-373-5178 or 800-228-2577.

Zanesville Visitors Center and Convention Bureau, 334 Shinnick Street, Zanesville, OH 43701. 614-453-5004 or 800-743-2303.

BLUE ROCK STATE PARK

Because it's off the beaten river trail, this small (335 acres) park is perfect for secluded walks among blue-gray shale. Once the site of hardscrabble farms, this land was deeded to the federal government under a resettlement program that gave Depression era families a chance to find a more productive life elsewhere. It was replanted in native trees and now forms a hilly, heavily wooded park with a small lake.

Where: Six and a half miles west of Duncan Falls, off County 45.

A white-tailed doe and fawn

Facilities: Camping, Rent-a-Camp (see page xx), ranger, boating (electric motors only), three miles of hiking trails, ten miles of bridle/hiking trails, beach, picnic tables, toilets, coin-operated showers at the beach, concession stand, part-time naturalist (shared with another park), nature programs. The park is open to campers and hikers all year. In winter, sledding, ice-skating, and ice fishing are popular.

For more information:
Blue Rock State Park, 7924 Cutler Lake Road, Blue Rock, OH 43720. 614-674-4794.

COSHOCTON

Best known for Roscoe Village, a restored canal town that re-creates the heyday of the Ohio and Erie Canal, Coshocton is found at the meeting of the Walhonding and Tuscarawas rivers, the start of the mighty Muskingum River. A ride aboard the horse-drawn *Monticello III* canal boat is a good way to get in the Muskingum mood. Then hike the paved path from Roscoe Village to the lake. It follows much of the original towpath and takes you past original locks and across a footbridge spanning the Walhonding.

Where: Roscoe Village is on US 36 in Coshocton. The towpath to Lake Park Recreation Area heads east from the village.
Facilities: Lake Park Recreation Area has picnicking, stables, a swimming area, a golf course, camping, boat rental, and a canoe livery and landing. The *Monticello III* operates Memorial Day through Labor Day and on weekends in shoulder seasons. For boat and park information, call 614-622-7528.
For more information:
Roscoe Village, 381 Hill Street, Coshocton, OH 43812. 614-622-9310 or 800-877-1830.

WOLF RUN STATE PARK

Located on Wolf Run Creek east of the Muskingum River is a 1,143-acre state park with a couple of special features that set it apart. It has its own runway and a fly-in camping area for pilots and their families. The terrain is ruggedly beautiful, centered by the deep, clear Wolf Run Lake and surrounded by craggy canyons, forests, and bush all atwitter with wild turkeys and grouse.

Where: Off I-77, east of the Belle Valley exit south of Cambridge, on State 215.
Facilities: Swimming area with changing rooms, rest rooms, picnic shelters, boat ramp, fishing, hill country camping (no electricity), showers, latrines, laundry, amphitheater with naturalist programs, runway and fly-in campground, nature center with small hiking trail. More ambitious hikers can take to the Buckeye Trail, which passes through the park.
For more information:
   Wolf Run State Park, Caldwell, OH 43724. 614-732-5035.

SENECAVILLE LAKE

The largest lake in the Muskingum Watershed Conservancy District, this 3,500-acre waterway is crowded on peak summer days, but its woods, trails, and campsites take you away from the beach crowds. Don't miss the national fish hatchery that is located here. Learn how fish are nurtured to replenish Ohio lakes and streams.

Where: Take the Belle Valley interchange off I-77 south of Cambridge. Go east on State 821, then left on State 215 to the park entrance on Bond Ridge Road.
Facilities: Cabins, camping, fishing, sandy swimming beach, boat rental and supplies, marina with restaurant, picnic shelters with grills, naturalist programs.
For more information:
   Senecaville Lake, 614-685-6013.

RECREATION LAND

Imagine a 30,000-acre green space planted since 1944 with 40 million tree seedlings. Imagine ponds and lakes set among the poplars, locusts, sycamores, cottonwoods, silver maples, black walnuts, and countless evergreens. Imagine fishing, hiking, camping, and hunting, all of it free.

It sounds too good to be true, but ReCreation Land is such a place. The Ohio Power Company, which serves electric customers in fifty-three of Ohio's eighty-eight counties, has reclaimed old strip mine land and turned it into this wilderness playground.

Lying 22 miles south of Zanesville and 28 miles north of Marietta, the land was never good for farming. Under layers of clay and limestone, however, are rich seams of coal that yield 5,000 or more tons per acre to stoke the generators that supply electricity to 627,000 Ohioans.

Much of the land today is heavily forested and dotted by some 350 small lakes and ponds. When new surface mining regulations were adopted in 1972, the reclamation emphasis turned from planting trees to planting grasses. Old forests are now separated by miles of pastureland and hay fields. A 2,800-acre preserve has been set aside for a Canada goose project and now hosts a flock of several thousand geese. The 1,500 acres of water are stocked with bass, bluegill, catfish, sunfish, northern pike, and other fish that are caught in record sizes.

Although the sense of wilderness is occasionally invaded by the sights and sounds of the work that goes on here, that, too, can be part of the show. Keep an eye out for Big Muskie, a dragline that weighs 27 million pounds and has a housing 6 stories high.

Where: ReCreation Land lies seventeen miles south of I-70, seven miles west of I-77, and eight miles east of McConnelsville.

Don't go, however, before you write the Ohio Power Company for a free permit.

Facilities: Eight campgrounds with campsites, picnic tables, latrines, and fireplaces; one site with picnic tables and latrines; one site with picnic tables, water, and latrines. The Buckeye Trail goes through ReCreation Land for about ten miles. Horseback camping is permitted in specified areas. The area is patrolled by park staff in cooperation with the county sheriff's department and the Ohio Division of Wildlife.

Special note: You must carry your permit with you at all times when you're on Ohio Power land. Without it, you could be arrested for trespassing. You'll also receive a map listing visitor rules and showing locations of picnic and camping sites, latrines, water taps, information centers, restricted areas, and public telephones. Only licensed road vehicles are permitted on Ohio Power land (no snowmobiles, all-terrain vehicles, or dune buggies). Boat motors must be 6 horsepower or less. Fishermen and hunters must have valid Ohio fishing and hunting licenses.

For more information:

Ohio Power Company, 301 Cleveland Avenue S.W., Canton, OH 44701.

13

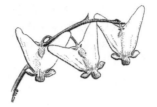

Mohican Country

Visitors to these green and giving hills know immediately why Pulitzer Prize–winning author and pioneer conservationist Louis Bromfield chose this area to establish his Malabar Farm: fields of Ohio soil, meadows on gentle slopes, forests to provide wood for building and burning, trees dripping with nuts to feed both people and a flourishing population of upland game.

Hikers and canoeists flock here from heavily populated Cleveland and Columbus for good reason. It's a year-round playground, as popular with skiers in winter as it is with avid boaters and campers in summer.

The Mohican River of 12,000 years ago flowed in the other direction and is thought to have ended at Hudson Bay. After it was blocked by a glacier, it cut a new route, reversed its course, and became an important trade outlet to New Orleans. In its agony, it gouged out the rushing Clear Fork and pooled into Pleasant Hill Lake.

In the rubble left behind by the mile-thick glacier were the seeds of today's rare plants plus a wealth of formations, quartz from the far north, and granite pushed down from the Canadian

Cambrian Shield. In some areas, southern species such as magnolias still remain from the tropical preglacial period. In others, towering hemlocks from the far north flourish.

All kinds of wildlife call the Mohican home. Wild turkeys, once almost unknown in this area, have been reintroduced. White-tailed deer, a variety of turtles, and a full array of fish are found. Especially abundant are bass and catfish in the river and bass and saugeye in Pleasant Hill Lake.

MALABAR FARM

The only operating farm located in an Ohio state park, Malabar was a labor of love for Louis Bromfield, who restored its tired soil, planted new trees and preserved the old, and taught an industrial generation the value of the vanishing land.

Today it's a working, teaching farm with a year-round calendar of events. In March, horse-drawn wagons take visitors to the sugar camp to see how maple syrup is made. In the spring, you can take a wildflower walk with a park ranger, then show up for spring plowing. It's a competition in which draft horses and teamsters compete.

Bluebirds are a special project of the farm, where several programs are held each year to teach visitors how to make bluebird nesting boxes and otherwise attract this vanishing species. Barn dances are held a couple of times a year. During pioneer encampments, interpretive characters demonstrate pioneer skills. At Christmas, Bromfield's thirty-two-room home is decorated for the holidays, which are celebrated with cookies, wassail, caroling, and horse-drawn wagon rides.

Where: Off I-71, head east on State 97 for seventeen miles.
Facilities: In addition to the farm and its activities, the state park offers two campgrounds (plus more than a dozen private

campgrounds in the nearby area), picnicking at several scenic sites, fishing, twelve miles of hiking trails, canoeing, restaurants, twenty-two miles of bridle trails, cabins, a resort lodge, a nature center, and an amphitheater where nature programs are held. Nearby Mohican Memorial State Forest offers backcountry camping at sites that cannot be reached by car.

Canoeing: For a list of canoe liveries on the Mohican River, call the Mansfield and Richland County Convention and Visitors Bureau, 419-525-1300 or 800-642-8282. Trips of two hours to six days can be arranged.

Special note: In addition to state park fees, an admission is charged to the Bromfield house. Its hours are more limited than those for the park itself. Call ahead to learn of scheduled events.

For more information:

Malabar Farm, 4050 Bromfield Road, Lucas, OH 44864. 419-892-2784.

Mohican Memorial State Forest, 3060 CR 939, Perrysville, OH 44864. 419-938-6222.

KINGWOOD CENTER

Once the baronial home and estate of an industrial magnate, Kingwood is a forty-seven-acre showplace of formal and display gardens. It is especially beautiful in spring, when the 40,000 tulips bloom in bursts of yellow, beds of red, and borders of white. But the show lasts all summer with the planting of 30,000 annuals among the perennials and ponds. Waterfowl watching is good here, too.

Where: From downtown, take Park Avenue west for about two miles.

Hours: Closed Monday and holidays. Hours vary seasonally. Call ahead.

Facilities: Mansion with horticultural library, rest rooms, walking paths, many special events.
For more information:
    Kingwood Center, 900 Park Avenue West, Mansfield, OH 44906. 419-522-0211.

FOWLER WOODS STATE NATURE PRESERVE

A retreating glacier took a pause here for perhaps a century or so, leaving gently rolling land with a thick deposit of till — a mixture of clay, boulders, sand, and gravel. A wondrous jumble of plants that the glacier had gathered up in its travels took root. Over the ages, they formed habitat for a 133-acre nature zoo: hawks and turkey vultures, barred owls, many types of non-venomous snakes (including the rare northern copper-belly), salamanders, turtles, chipmunks, squirrels, and much more.

Climb the observation tower and look out over the forests and sedge meadow. The woods are especially popular in spring and early summer during wildflower bloom.

Where: From Olivesburg, which is west of Ashland and northeast of Mansfield, go six miles northwest on Olivesburg-Fitchville Road.
Facilities: Observation tower, 2 miles of nature trails, 7,500-foot boardwalk, wheelchair access.
For more information:
    Fowler Woods State Nature Preserve, 419-265-6453.

CHARLES MILL LAKE

Found just off I-71 east of Mansfield, Charles Mill Lake is a shallow, 1,350-acre lake surrounded by 2,000 acres of parkland.

Its fishing is fabulous—channel catfish, bullheads, crappies, yellow perch, and the like—and its pontoon rental fleet is popular. Bring your own boat if you like, as long as its engine isn't larger than 10 horsepower. The lake's annual boat parade in August is splashy, clean fun.

Where: West of State 603 and south of US 30.
Facilities: Camping, launch ramp, playground, scheduled cruise boat rides, nature hikes, picnic area with grills, rest rooms, food service, swimming area with lifeguard, rangers, boat rental.
For more information:
    Park, 419-368-6885; marina, 419-368-5951.
    Convention and Visitors Bureau, 52 Park Avenue West, Mansfield, OH 44902. 419-525-1300 or 800-642-8282.

PLEASANT HILL LAKE

Pleasant Hill Lake, just west of Perrysville on State 95, is an 850-acre reservoir with no horsepower limit. It's richly stocked, thanks to the fisheries management experts at the Ohio Division of Wildlife. So launch your boat, hurry out to the honey hole, and spend the day matching wits with catfish, bass, walleye, and saugeye.

Where: On State 95, one-fifth mile west of Perrysville.
Facilities: Beach with lifeguard, rangers, activities, nature center, playground, marina, camping, cabins, food supplies, concession stand at beach, hiking trails, airstrip.
For more information:
    Pleasant Hill Lake, 419-938-7884.

14

Southeastern Ohio

Wayne National Forest is only part of the green-gold that covers much of southeastern Ohio, the state's Appalachia. Thousands of acres of land outside the forest are also public lands in state and county parks, preserves, state forests, and reserves. It adds up to one of the Midwest's most rugged, wildly beautiful, and varied green spaces, a paradise of woods and water, deer and grouse, songbirds and silence.

WAYNE NATIONAL FOREST

It isn't easy to get a handle on Wayne National Forest because, unlike the grand national parks and forests out west, this is a piecemeal property in three major, and a few minor, chunks in southeastern Ohio. Although it's a patchwork, it adjoins state parks, enwraps state forests, and hopscotches between city parks. And it's growing each year as funds and properties become available.

    You won't find much in the way of facilities in the national forest itself, but thanks to the configuration of the property, most of its pieces are surrounded by roads, settlements, and other lightly populated areas where you can find a country store here and a canoe livery there with plenty of campgrounds in between.

The easternmost portion of the forest covers parts of Monroe, Noble, and Washington counties on the north side of the Ohio River. This section runs roughly from Hannibal south almost to Marietta. It is bordered on the north by Lewisville and Woodsfield.

Another chunk rambles through the area northwest of Athens. A third piece spreads across Gallia, Lawrence, and Scioto counties. By looking at the map, you can clearly see its origins. As old farms fall into disuse and are offered for sale, they are added bit by bit to the national treasure. At last count, Wayne National Forest covered 178,000 acres.

The full variety of southern Ohio field and forest can be found here, from new-growth forests on recently abandoned farmlands to wild orchids cradled in undergrowth that may never have been seen before by human eyes.

One of the most interesting bridle trails in the forest is an eighteen-mile loop between Gore and Shawnee known as the Stone Church Horse Trail. Just north of the trailhead (on private property) is the skeleton of St. Peter's Catholic Church, which was once a thriving congregation of 100 members. The first Mass celebrated in this area was offered by Dominican priests to the Indians and pioneers who came to nearby Salt Run. In the church's cemetery are more than 100 gravestones, some dating to the mid-1800s. According to legend, a plague wiped out the little community, and the church fell to ruin.

One of the best ways for backpackers to sample the forest is to hike the thirteen-mile Wildcat Hollow Trail loop through one of southern Ohio's remotest tangles astride Irish Ridge. Find the trailhead on County 58 off State 13 south of Hatfield, on the border of Perry and Morgan counties.

The trail takes you past some of the small, quietly pumping oil wells that are still common in the Ohio hills, through dense elm and hickory forests, and past an old one-room school and a farmhouse. This isn't a trail to take when you're in a hurry. Make camp early to watch throughout the twilight for wild rabbits, woodchucks, quail, and deer. In the morning, give the forest creatures time to come out before you begin banging skillets and boiling coffee. You may see grouse and raccoons, opossums, and more deer before you hit the trail.

Enjoy the soaring ridges and stream bottoms, plantations of white pines, open meadows, and bold rock formations. Some of the trail is along old roadbeds, built at the price of unimaginable toil by early homesteaders. This part of the forest coincides with (or borders) popular Burr Oak State Park, which has many hiking trails, primitive and developed camping, a lodge, and much more.

Also passing through a seventeen-mile stretch of the forest near New Straitsville is a segment of the North Country National Scenic Trail, whose designers dropped this far south only because of the area's irresistible beauty. It's a hike of about nine hours.

Where: Before tackling any of this territory, get topographic maps and other appropriate guides from the forest supervisor at Wayne-Hoosier National Forest. Request a state index map showing topographic quad maps from the U.S. Geological Survey Map Information Office, Denver, CO 80225. Also contact district rangers at Athens Ranger District, Ironton Ranger District, and Marietta Unit.

Facilities: Within the forest are five campgrounds with two to sixty-seven sites. Drinking water is available at three sites, swimming at one, boating and canoeing at five, horse trails at two, and hiking trails at six, some of them as long as twenty-five

Opossum twins

miles. One site is accessible to people with physical impairments. The statewide Buckeye Trail and the North Country Trail go through the forest. Backpackers are invited to explore almost any of the undeveloped areas of the park.

Hours: Day sites are open all year during daylight hours, but some campgrounds and boat docks are closed in the winter.

Camping: Some units in the forest can be reserved via credit card through Mistix, 800-283-CAMP. Most are on a first-come basis. Located in the Athens District is the Burr-Oak Cove Campground, offering nineteen primitive sites with no water. A modest fee is charged. Oak Hill and Iron Ridge campgrounds in the Ironton District have some electric hookups and charge accordingly. Backpack camping is permitted anywhere on Wayne National Forest land. As long as you stay on the trail, you're on public land. Many pockets of private land are beside or inside trail loops, so don't venture far afield.

Special note: Nonburnable trash should be carried out. Garbage and human waste can be buried in the rich soil, where it will quickly decompose. Permits are not required for backpacking or building campfires. Small portable stoves are preferred, but carefully positioned and tended campfires are permitted.

Caution: Small streams can swell quickly in heavy rains. Avoid snakes and poison ivy.

For more information:

Forest Supervisor, Wayne-Hoosier National Forest, 3527 Tenth Street, Bedford, IN 47421. 812-275-5987.

Athens Ranger District, 219 Columbus Road, Athens, OH 45701. 614-592-6644.

Ironton Ranger District, 710 Park Avenue, Ironton, OH 45638. 614-532-3223.

Marietta Unit, Route 1, Box 132, Marietta, OH 45750. 614-373-9055.

LAKE VESUVIUS RECREATION AREA

Lake Vesuvius Recreation Area at Ellisonville lies within Wayne National Forest. Here you can see a restored iron furnace, a relic from the days before Cleveland and Youngstown replaced southern Ohio as the steelmaking giant. During the Civil War, Ohio foundries armed the Union with cannons and shot; today the industry here is just a memory.

Where: Off State 93 between Ironton and Pedro.
Facilities: Camping, fishing, hiking, boating, nature center, bridle trails.
Special note: Just north of Pedro, also off State 93, is the 2,745-acre Dean State Forest, which also lies within Wayne National Forest. There are no facilities except for a twenty-mile bridle trail. For information, contact Dean State Forest, Route 1, Pedro, OH 45659.
For more information:
   Lake Vesuvius Recreation Area, 614-532-0151.

ZALESKI STATE FOREST

Adjoining Wayne National Forest north of Zaleski and west of Athens is a 26,313-acre wilderness managed by the Ohio Division of Forestry. Like other state forests, it is cut and reclaimed, planted and preserved for the best benefit of both recreational and environmental interests. Two state forest nurseries produce 7 million to 9 million seedlings a year for the use of foresters and homeowners.

   Hiking the twenty-three-mile walking trail and thirty-three-mile bridle trail is free. This is one of the gentler paths, said to be less strenuous hiking than the sixty-mile backpack trail in Shawnee State Forest. Self-register twenty-four hours a day.

Where: Take State 93 south off US 33. Continue through Mount Pleasant, then turn east onto State 56. Call ahead for maps of the forest. The backpack trailhead is at Hope Furnace on State 278 south of State 56.
Facilities: Hiking trail, bridle trail, horseback camp (no drinking water), backpack camping with latrines and water.
For more information:
Zaleski State Forest, Zaleski, OH 45698. 614-596-5781.

LAKE HOPE STATE PARK

Adjoining Zaleski State Forest is Lake Hope State Park, which has hiking trails, a swimming beach, a beaver population that puts on a nonstop show, boating (electric motors only), a restaurant, picnic areas with drinking water and toilets, boat rental, a bridle trail, and full-facilities camping. A popular lodge that sleeps eight must be reserved months in advance.

Where: Take State 278 south from Nelsonville for thirteen miles.
Facilities: As described. For dining reservations, call 614-596-4117.
For more information:
Lake Hope State Park, Zaleski, OH 45698. 614-596-5253.

SYMMES CREEK

Two loop trails—Symmes Creek Trail and Morgan Sisters Trail—are located on both sides of Symmes Creek. They wind through a rugged, ridged section of the Ironton District of Wayne National Forest and are connected by a short trail at the creek. Combined, they make a fourteen-mile overnight hike through heavy woods, up and down rocky outcroppings, through overgrown fields, and across unspoiled wetlands. The variety of vegetation and wildlife is among the best to be seen in the state.

Where: Head west from Gallipolis on State 141, passing Symmes Creek and Gage roads to turn right onto Woodside Road. Follow the signs to the trailhead. Write ahead to the national forest for topo maps.

RACCOON CREEK COUNTY PARK

Although it's not quite in Wayne National Forest, this Gallia County park offers some of the developed recreation facilities that outdoors-loving families sometimes look for. If the ball fields and picnic shelters are too busy for your taste, hie to the nature trails through wetlands and meadows, woods and a craggy gorge.

Walk softly as you watch for ruffed grouse, wild turkeys, white-tailed deer, foxes, and raccoons. The official park flower is the trillium, which blankets the moist woodlands in spring, but you'll also find a rare plant called the reflexed umbrella sedge.

Where: From Gallipolis, take State 141 west. Turn left onto State 775, then right onto Dan Jones Road. From US 35, take State 325 south, then turn left onto State 141 and right onto Dan Jones Road. The park is in Patriot, pronounced "PAT-ree-ut."
Hours: Open 9:00 A.M. to sunset except Sunday, when the park opens at 10:00 A.M.
Facilities: Baseball diamonds, playing fields, picnicking, reservation-only picnic shelters with electricity and water,

MEIGS COUNTY

If you drew a line on the map from the Ironton District of Wayne National Forest to the eastern end of the Athens District, it would fall just north of one of the state's most wildly exciting drives along the Big Bend in the Ohio River. Wild ups and downs along the river on State 124 and State 338 take you to two pretty wilderness areas that are just a jump downstream from Blennerhassett Island. Although it's claimed as a West Virginia tourist attraction, this island is where Aaron Burr holed up after shooting Alexander Hamilton in a duel. The mansion where Burr and Harman Blennerhassett are said to have discussed a plan to overthrow the government was once an overgrown ruin but has been meticulously restored.

Meigs County history goes back to its first settlement in 1796 at Letart Falls. Its county courthouse is the state's oldest, dating to 1822. The famous Morgan's Raid, the only time Ohio was invaded during the Civil War, raged through this area. Today this county's parks are some of the best finds in the state.

two-mile fitness trail, hiking trails, tennis, playground, volleyball, rest rooms. In progress is the building of a twenty-eight-mile rails-to-trails biking and hiking pathway that will run along the old Black Diamond Coal railroad right-of-way through the park. It should open by 1996 or 1997.

For more information:

Raccoon Creek County Park, 614-446-4612, ext. 256.

Ohio Valley Visitors Center, 45 State Street, Gallipolis, OH 45631. 614-446-6882.

FORKED RUN STATE PARK

Locally pronounced "For-KED Run," this 715-acre park centers on 102-acre Forked Run Lake. It's located in the nonglaciated portion of Ohio, in terrain that ranges from rich bottomland, to cliffs that reach 160 feet along the river, and to inland hills a thousand feet high. Here the careful observer can see where the damming of ancient rivers by glacial ice created a new drainage system and changed the face of Ohio thousands of years ago.

Forked Run is a boating bonanza, opening on both the lake and the Ohio River. Swim off the sandy beach, picnic, or take to the nature trails to look for sweet, syrupy persimmons (leave them for the bears, please), bananalike papaws, meaty acorns, and all the wildlife of an Ohio countryside, plus impressive views of the lake and river.

Where: On State 124 in Reedsville.
Facilities: Boating on the Ohio River and, with a 10-horsepower limit, on the lake; picnicking; boat rental and ramp; campground; Rent-a-Camp (see page xx); four miles of challenging hiking trails. The 2,601 acres of Shade River State Forest are a forestry management and hunting preserve with no other facilities.
For more information:
Forked Run State Park, P.O. Box 127, Reedsvillle, OH 45772. 614-378-6206.

MONROE COUNTY
Soaring hills rise out of the Ohio River to form rugged forests, craggy cliffs, deep canyons with rushing creeks, and smoky lookouts. You won't see snowcapped mountains in Monroe County, and perhaps it's stretching things a mite for it to call itself the "Switzerland of Ohio." Still, this sparsely populated county south of I-70 and east of I-77 is one of the state's greenest and most fetching frontiers.

More than half the county lies within Wayne National Forest, and most of the rest is wilderness that drains into the Little Muskingum River, which enters the Ohio at Marietta.

SUNFISH CREEK STATE FOREST

Looking across from West Virginia to the point where Sunfish Creek meets the Ohio River, you can see this 637-acre timber management area with no facilities except trails used by hunters. Although the forest has no designated bridle trails, riding is permitted on forest roads. The terrain is steep, rising sharply from the river.

Sunfish Creek can be canoed most of its length from the County 27 bridge northwest of Woodsfield, although some portages may be necessary and may require the permission of landowners. Roadside parking at the creek can be found at the County 27 bridge, the State 26 bridge northeast of Monroesville, the County 29/6 bridge west of Cameron, and the State 78 bridge in Clarington.

Where: Off State 7 between Clarington (State 78) and Powhatan Point.
Facilities: None.
Canoeing: Request "Boating on Ohio's Streams, Section 4" (Southeast), from the Division of Watercraft, 1952 Belcher Drive, Building C-2, Columbus, OH 43224-1386. 614-265-6480.
For more information:
Division of Forestry, Fountain Square, Columbus, OH 43224. 614-265-6694.

MONROE LAKE AND WILDLIFE AREA

A 38-acre lake that is stocked annually with trout is the focal point of this 1,293-acre, darkly wooded green space. One of eastern Ohio's best-kept secrets, this wildlife area is overshadowed by Senecaville Lake, which is larger and closer to the cities.

Where: From I-70 east of Cambridge, take State 800 for about twenty miles.
Facilities: Fishing, camping, picnic area, rest rooms.
For more information:
Monroe County Park District, Room 34, Monroe County Courthouse, Woodsfield, OH 43793. 614-472-1328.

PIATT PARK

Ohio's underground is laced with caves, but because most of the best-known caves are commercial attractions, we decided not to highlight them in this green guide. Piatt Park's unexploited gorges and caverns are, by contrast, set in a wooded 119-acre park whose only price of admission is a yen to commune with the sylvan silence.

Where: Four miles east of Woodsfield off State 78.
Facilities: Camping, picnicking, latrines.
For more information:
Monroe County Park District, Room 34, Monroe County Courthouse, Woodsfield, OH 43793. 614-472-1328.

RING MILL

Ring Mill is little more than another canoe access point on the Little Muskingum River, but the Ring Stone House here is on the National Register of Historic Places. Come sit by the river and spread a picnic in an idyllic setting. The little park lies within Wayne National Forest, near a covered bridge.

To canoe the entire 69.7-mile length of the Little Muskingum, which has no portages or restricted areas, put in at Ring

Mill. The last takeout before the Ohio River is at County 9/333 east of Marietta and south of Dell.

Where: On County 68 off State 26 in Washington Township.
Facilities: Picnic tables, camping, rest rooms.
Canoeing: Request "Boating on Ohio's Streams, Section 4" (Southeast), from the Division of Watercraft, 1952 Belcher Drive, Building C-2, Columbus OH, 43224-1386. 614-265-6480. Always get current state-of-the-river reports locally before launching.
For more information:

Monroe County Park District, Room 34, Monroe County Courthouse, Woodsfield, OH 43793. 614-472-1328.

15

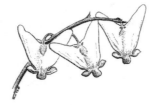

Sandusky River Valley

Designated a state scenic river from Upper Sandusky to Fremont, seventy miles downstream, the Sandusky River winds past dolomite and sandstone outcroppings and through some of the most bountiful farmland in Ohio. Its northern reaches go through flat and gently rolling areas that were once the shorelines of lakes formed as the glaciers receded. In the south, its shores are broken ridges up to fifty feet high, moraines deposited by advancing ice packs.

When white settlers arrived on the scene, the riverbanks were the home of the Seneca and Wyandot Indians. The Wyandots held out until 1843, when they, like other eastern Indians, were forced to move westward. One of the four major forts built here by the pioneers, Fort Stephenson, was the site of an important U.S. victory in the War of 1812.

Get a map showing points on the scenic portion of the river, then interpret it according to whether you'll be traveling by water or road. Canoeing the river takes you through waters that range from Class 1 to Class 4. The main highway from Upper Sandusky to Fremont is State 53. From it, you can reach the river access points that are part of the scenic river greenbelt.

The Sandusky is a favorite with fishermen, especially during annual migrations of walleye and white bass from Sandusky Bay to the Ballville Dam. Visitors find beauty in the river at any time of year, however.

For more information:

Fremont/Sandusky County Convention and Visitors Bureau, 1510 East State Street, Fremont, OH 43420. 800-255-8070.

RIVERSIDE PARKS

Indian Mill State Memorial is a historic site off US 23 on County 50N north of Upper Sandusky. Housing a museum of milling, it was named Indian Mill because the first mill on this site was built by the government for use by the Wyandot Indians. The site has picnicking and rest rooms.

Another river access point that has rest rooms is **Abbott Bridge,** near Old Fort off State 53 on Township 152. **Wolf Creek** on State 53 south of Fremont has a campground, picnicking, and rest rooms.

Harrison Smith Park, off US 23 in Upper Sandusky (take State 53/67 to Wyandot Street East), offers picnicking, fishing, swimming, and rest rooms. To get to **Hecks Bridge** and **Howard Collier Picnic Area,** take County 58 east from McCutchenville to Township 131N, then go east on Township 38.

Nature Trails Park is in Tiffin. Take State 53 to East Davis Street. **Portage Trail Park,** located south of Fremont, is on County 132, off State 53. **Roger Young Memorial Park** is in Fremont. Take US 20 to the Rawson Street exit. Follow West

State Street to South Front Street and turn east along the river. The park has picnic tables and rest rooms.

Wolf Creek Park is located south of Fremont off State 53. This ninety-three-acre park has a playground, primitive camping, well water, pit toilets, picnic tables and grills, and nature trails along the Sandusky. The Buckeye Trail winds through the park. Just west of the park on County 9 is an old covered bridge across Wolf Creek. Built in 1851, it's the last remaining covered bridge in northwestern Ohio.

PICKEREL CREEK WILDLIFE AREA

Some of the finest wetlands remaining in Ohio can be found in this 2,106-acre preserve, which is half open grassland and half woods, brush, or marsh. Pickerel Creek, a high-quality freshwater habitat, abounds in bullheads, crappies, channel catfish, freshwater drums, yellow perch, northern pike, and the occasional bowfin and longnose gar. Waterfowl, which had gradually abandoned the area as the wetlands were drained and the wild rice disappeared, have come back by the flock.

Bird-watchers are rewarded with a long list of sightings, especially during spring and fall migrations. Watch for mallard, wood ducks, black ducks, blue- and green-winged teal, and sometimes wigeon, pintail, gadwalls, and shovelers. Whistling swans, Canada geese, great blue herons, pheasant, and countless common songbirds also have been sighted.

Rabbits hop among the old fencerows, and muskrat roam freely in the marsh and along the creek. It's likely that the patient observer will see plenty of deer and raccoons, as well as the occasional mink, woodchuck, deer, and opossum.

Where: Between Sandusky Bay and US 6, bounded by Township

A raccoon

254 and Township 280. The check-in station is off Township 256 at the bay. Three parking areas are found along US 6.

Special note: This is a public hunting area, so be aware of when hunting seasons are in effect.

For more information:

Pickerel Creek Wildlife Area, 419-547-6007.

Department of Natural Resources, 925 Lima Avenue, Findlay, OH 45840. 419-424-5000.

KILLDEER PLAINS

Prairie and marsh team up to make this 8,000-acre reserve a smorgasbord of wildlife, from waterfowl to upland birds and game that make their home around the reservoir. Wildlife watching, hunting, fishing, and nonmotorized boating are popular. Except during local, regional, and national dog trials, it's a quiet wilderness where you may even spot one of the bald eagles that nest here.

Where: West of the Little Sandusky River and about eleven miles southwest of Upper Sandusky between Harpster and Marseilles. The reservoir is on State 67 at Marseilles; the rest of the wildlife area is strung across the area south of County 71.

For more information:

Killdeer Plains, 614-496-2254.

Department of Natural Resources, 925 Lima Avenue, Findlay, OH 45840. 419-424-5000.

16

Hocking River Valley

Athens and the campus of mammoth Ohio University are cradled by a bend in the Hocking River. In season, the student population swells little Athens by tens of thousands, but it all adds to the sophisticated, rural charm of this corner of Appalachia. Rimmed with rivers and creeks, and half surrounded by Wayne National Forest—13,500 acres of it in Athens County alone—Athens and Hocking counties are among Ohio's most rugged and exciting outdoor playlands.

For more information:

Hocking County Tourism Association, Box 350, Logan, OH 43138. 800-589-7503.

Athens County Convention and Visitors Bureau, Box 1019, Athens, OH 45701. 614-592-1819 or 800-878-9767.

Wayne National Forest, 219 Columbus Road, Athens, OH 45701. 614-592-6644.

ATHENS

This is a university town, and that means a great zest for nature and the outdoors. Try the three-mile jogging and bike path that follows the river on campus between the Richland Avenue and Stimson Avenue bridges and beyond in both directions. Then take a walking tour of the historic College Green. The walk takes you past stately buildings that date to as early as 1818 and under trees a century old. Behind the library in the Wolfe Memorial Garden, sit in the shade of leafy sweet gum trees, pink and white dogwoods, and magnolias. It's a peaceful pocket on a busy campus.

Where: Athens is located at the intersection of US 33 and US 50. The College Green is bounded by South Court, East Union, University Terrace, and Park Place. The self-guided tour begins at the corner of College Street and East Union, where you can pick up the descriptive brochure at Baker Center.
Facilities: University facilities, nearby shopping and dining.
For more information:
Athens County Convention and Visitors Bureau, P.O. Box 1019, Athens, OH 45701. 614-592-1819 or 800-878-9767.

CRADLE IN THE ROCK

Rock formations in the Hocking Hills come thirteen to the dozen, but this sweetly sculptured series of small, sheltering caves is worth discovering. It's little known, so you're on your own to find it. The caves are formed of Buffalo sandstone, which lies over Brush Creek limestone. They're on the north end of Fox Lake, a 421-acre wildlife area roamed by deer, grouse, squirrels, rabbits, quail, and woodchucks.

Where: Four miles west of Athens, off US 50 or State 56. Take County 10 to County 19 to Fox Lake.
Facilities: None. This is a wildlife area used by hunters and fishermen.
For more information:

Athens County Convention and Visitors Bureau, P.O. Box 1019, Athens, OH 45701. 614-592-1819 or 800-878-9767.

SMOKE RISE HORSEMAN'S CAMPGROUND

A 2,000-acre family-owned business, this unique equestrian resort in the Hocking Hills is surrounded by Wayne National Forest and the Trimble Wildlife Area. Bridle trails wind for miles through the forested hills. At night, camp in a tent at a primitive site or in an RV with hookups and enjoy the company of other horseback campers. If you don't have a horse, you can rent one. Organized trail rides are offered several times a year. Rates include camping, meals, a hayride, and a barn dance.

Where: Take US 33 to Nelsonville, then take State 78 to Murray City. The first road on the left is County 92. Turn left and go 1.5 miles to the Smoke Rise entrance.
Facilities: Primitive or hookup camping, horse rental, stables and tack, trail rides, activities, tennis, swimming pool.
For more information:

Smoke Rise Horseman's Campground, 82 North Court Street, Athens, OH 45701. 614-592-4077 or 614-762-9533.

STROUDS RUN STATE PARK

Built at a spring that has been an Ohio landmark since the first settlers drank its rushing waters, this state park sprawls over

2,606 acres and offers a 161-acre spring-fed lake. Set among mature oaks, beeches, hickories, and sycamores, the park is too busy when day-trippers spill in from Columbus. However, they tend to cluster at the north end of the lake, where most of the facilities are, ignoring the thirteen miles of trails that follow the tortuous shoreline and climb into the hills to overlooks and the site of a pioneer cemetery. The crowding coincides with the school year, which means unexpectedly small attendance on many summer days when college students have left Athens and Columbus.

Where: Off US 50 east of Athens.

Facilities: Boating with a 10-horsepower limit, boat launch, boat rental, fishing, swimming beach and changing rooms, picnicking, toilets, primitive camping, Rent-a-Camp (see page xx), amphitheater with programs, hiking and bridle trails.

For more information:

Strouds Run State Park, 11661 State Park Road, Athens, OH 47501. 614-592-2302.

HOCKING HILLS STATE PARK

"Am I still in Ohio?" ask wide-eyed visitors as they see the dramatic sandstone and shale, cliffs and canyons, caves and waterfalls. *Ohio Magazine* picked this region as having Ohio's best rock scenery, most photogenic waterfall, and best caves.

The park covers 2,000 acres, but that's only a fraction of the total park acreage in this area, which is almost entirely state and national forest, nature preserves, private campgrounds, and other green space.

More than 7,000 years ago, Adena Indians hunted these forested gorges and found shelter in the shallow caves. Later Indians called it Hockhocking, meaning "bottle," for the bottlelike

A chipmunk in the chokecherries

shape that the river took on when it was blocked by glacial ice. Wind and flowing waters shaped the sandstone, creating deep recesses now known as Ash Cave, Old Man's Cave, and the 150-foot-high Cantwell Cliffs.

Mill owners moved to the Hocking River in the early 1800s to set up mills to grind grain, saw lumber, and weave woolens. By 1870, the caves were already a tourist attraction. Cedar Falls is stunning in springtime and impressive even in winter when the water slows to a trickle. When icicles form on the steep cliffs, the park becomes a fairyland. Pushed south by the glaciers (which never quite reached this area), seeds of Canadian hemlock took root. Early settlers mistook the trees for cedars, hence the name of the falls in this hemlock forest.

In the deeply wooded gorge, you'll see the largest tree in Ohio, a hemlock 149 feet tall and 46 inches around. Also look for Saltpeter Cave, where early settlers mined saltpeter for use in gunpowder.

Hocking State Forest is managed for harvest as well as for recreation. Its trees protect watersheds, hold soils, and may be logged for pulp, firewood, or veneer. State foresters have selected an interesting variety of trees for those who love to hike among them, photographing and identifying them. You can view Virginia and pitch pines, sassafras trees, oaks, hemlocks, beeches, black birches, red and sugar maples, yellow poplars, white ashes, basswood trees, and hickories. Whole plantations of red, white, and shortleaf pines have been developed by planting seedlings on abandoned farmland.

The 1,200-mile Buckeye Trail passes through the park. One section of it, the Grandma Gatewood Trail, offers a six-mile hike from the trailhead at the Upper Falls at Old Man's Cave to Cedar Falls and Ash Cave. Grandma Gatewood was an elderly Ohio woman who set out one day to hike the Appalachian Trail alone, carrying only a blanket and a knife. Quietly, she logged most of America's most ambitious hikes.

CONKLE'S HOLLOW STATE NATURE PRESERVE
Also in the Hocking Hills is Conkle's Hollow State Nature Preserve,
which has fourteen miles of trails, rest rooms, an observation tower,
and drinking water. Moist and green, it's especially well-known for
its lavish spring wildflower show of white trilliums, purple rocket,
bloodroot, Dutchman's-breeches, and chickweed.

Where: Take US 33 from Columbus or Athens, then turn south
onto State 374. The park office is on State 664. State forest headquarters and the state forest rapelling area are off State 374.

Facilities: Campground with swimming pool for campers' use
only, primitive camping, fishing lake, cabins, twenty-four miles
of hiking trails (including the wheelchair-accessible Ash Cave
Trail), picnic tables with grills, latrines, drinking water, dining
lodge with swimming pool (fee), visitors center with naturalist,
nature programs, cabins, game room. State forest facilities
include fifteen miles of bridle trails, a horseback camp, and a
rapelling area. The Buckeye Trail goes through the forest and
park. An especially pretty portion of the trail is the Grandma
Gatewood Trail.

Special note: The swimming pool, game room, and restaurant
are open in season only.

For more information:

Hocking Hills State Park, 20160 State 664, Logan, OH
43138. 614-385-6841.

Hocking Hills State Forest, 19275 State 374, Rockbridge,
OH 43149. 614-385-4402.

ROCKBRIDGE STATE NATURE PRESERVE

The state's largest natural bridge is accessible here by canoe or
on foot (although most of the trail is also wheelchair accessible).

The 100-acre, heavily wood preserve is a haven for birds as well as a prime place for spotting spring wildflowers. The 100-foot span, looming 45 feet over the river gorge below, was formed by nature out of Black Hand sandstone.

Where: Off US 33 southeast of Rockbridge, on Township 503 between State 180 and the roadside rest area.
Facilities: A 1.75-mile trail and 200-foot boardwalk.
For more information:
Rockbridge State Nature Preserve, 614-653-2541.

CANOEING THE HOCKING RIVER

Canoe this gentle river to get the best views of wooded banks alight with redbud, cliffy shale shorelines, and the timeless river itself. Outfitting can be supplied for a one- to two-hour trip from Crockets Run to Livery; a three- to four-hour paddle past the natural bridge from Clear Creek to Livery; an eleven-day trip from Logan to Nelsonville; or a three-day canoe and camping trip from Rush Creek to Nelsonville.

For more information:
Hocking Valley Canoe Livery, 32151 Chieftain Drive, Logan, OH 43138. 800-686-0386.

LAKE LOGAN STATE PARK

Consider it almost a part of Hocking Hills State Park because a 17-mile hiking trail connects the two. With 300 acres of land and 417 acres of water, this is a boating, fishing, and swimming park. Thanks to the large water area, it's also a good spot for observing nesting and resting birds: Canada geese, mallard, green and great blue herons, American egrets, kingfishers, wood ducks, and even the occasional seagull.

Where: Off US 33 west of Logan, on Lake Logan Road.
Facilities: Swimming area and beach with lifeguards; picnic shelters; concession stand open in summer; latrines; boat rental, fuel, and launch (10-horsepower limit).
For more information:
    Lake Logan State Park, 30443 Lake Logan Road, Logan, OH 43138. 614-385-3444.

17

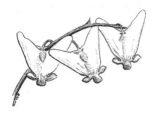

The Dells
of St. Marys

The interstates have passed by Van Wert and Mercer counties, which open to the vast plains of Indiana. That's good news for those who love the wide-open spaces of spots such as the St. Marys River and Grand Lake St. Marys, the largest man-made lake in Ohio.

It was only a few miles southwest of here along the Wabash River that two of the most important Indian battles in Ohio history were won and lost. Just after the Revolutionary War, General Arthur St. Clair's forces were bushwhacked by braves led by Indian heroes Little Turtle and Blue Jacket. Only a quarter of the Americans survived. Two years later, General "Mad Anthony" Wayne picked the same spot to build a big stockade and blockhouse complex. In a rushed and decisive effort, he threw together Fort Recovery in a week, beat the Indians at the Battle of Fallen Timbers, and saved Ohio from becoming a part of British Ontario.

The placid St. Marys seeps out of Auglaize County and becomes enough of a river to offer its first canoe access point at Memorial Park, off Chestnut Street in the community of St. Marys. A Class 1 river, which means easygoing, it can be canoed for most of its placid sixty-mile length.

One of the best places to view or enter the river is the Fort Adams Canoe Livery off the State 127 bridge west of Mendon. The site offers parking, picnicking, rest rooms, drinking water, camping, and canoe rental.

For more information:

Van Wert Area Convention and Visitors Bureau, 118 West Main Street, Van Wert, OH 45891. 419-238-4390.

GRAND LAKE ST. MARYS STATE PARK

Digging reservoirs and canals by hand was common in nineteenth-century Ohio, when German immigrants were paid a little more than a dollar a week and a daily ration of grog to create a massive, 13,500-acre lake to supply water to the Miami and Erie Canal. The canal in turn was part of an incredible complex that linked the Ohio River and Lake Erie.

A depth of at least five feet was required in the canals to float barges laden with goods that flowed out of Ohio farms and into the hungry markets to the north and south. So engineers designed a huge network of lakes, streams, locks, reservoirs, and aqueducts to supply the millions of gallons of water required to keep the canals at suitable levels.

The canals' heyday lasted only a few decades before railroads rushed through the state, carrying goods to market at heady speeds that mule-drawn barges could not begin to match. This gargantuan warren of waterways, as well as many of the waterfront towns that depended on the canals for their existence, were doomed. Their legacy, however, is a network of greenbelts—the canals and their towpaths—that extends for miles with only a hamlet here and an old lock or dam there. Many parts of the canals and feeders have been lost under cities and highways, of course, but others have been brought back as recreation areas and still others remain shrouded in undergrowth as they wait to be rediscovered by hikers and bicyclists.

Only 500 acres of this state park are land. All eyes are on the lake. Although unlimited horsepower is permitted and the lake is popular among powerboat operators, it has a colorful and active sailing community, too. Dotted with sailboats, with a real lighthouse supplying a backdrop, it's a favorite spot of photographers. Fishermen revel in fine catches of saugeye, bass, and northern pike, thanks to a state fish hatchery on the lake. Local crappie fishing is legendary.

Fish to your heart's content, or walk the lakefront to watch for waterfowl and songbirds. The park doesn't offer hiking trails as such, but with fifty-two miles of shoreline, you're never at a loss for a hike.

Where: South of US 33, about ten miles west of Wapakoneta. It's west of the community of St. Marys, off State 703.
Facilities: Swimming beaches with lifeguards, fishing, picnic shelters, boat rental and launch, campsites with electricity, showers, flush toilets, Rent-a-Camp (see page xx), nature programs. Supplies are easily obtained in surrounding settlements.
Special note: Visitors are welcome at the state fish hatchery, where warm- and cool-water hatches and fish-rearing ponds nurture millions of fingerling bass, pike, saugeye, catfish, and other fish that are introduced into nearby lakes and streams. For information, call 419-394-5170.
For more information:
Grand Lake St. Marys State Park, 834 Edgewater Drive, St. Marys, OH 45885. 419-394-3611.

LAKE LORAMIE STATE PARK

Loramie Creek is not in the St. Marys watershed but instead flows into the Great Miami River and on to the Ohio. Named for an ex-missionary who was defrocked, threw in his lot with the Indians, and went west, Lake Loramie State Park comprises a 1,650-acre lake surrounded by 400 acres of land.

Another legacy of the canal system, the pencil-thin lake has miles of meandering shoreline that curves into hidden coves. It's a speedboater's mecca, but the lake also has quiet, no-wake areas where canoeing is popular.

A nesting ground for great blue herons has been established on the lake, and an inland bluebird trail has attracted a colony of these popular birds. Park rangers have planted a patch of prairie grasses, and the Buckeye Trail also passes through.

Where: Off I-75, take State 119 west, then State 362 south.
Facilities: Fishing, swimming beach with lifeguards on peak days, picnic tables with grills, camping with hookups, Rent-a-Camp (see page xx), nature center, playgrounds, programs, cross-country skiing, sledding, ice fishing.
For more information:
Lake Loramie State Park, 11221 State 362, Minster, OH 45856-9311. 513-295-2011.

TECUMSEH NATURAL AREA AND ARBORETUM

The 200-acre Tecumseh Natural Area and Arboretum is on Ohio State University's Lima campus. Laced with walking paths, the stand of deciduous trees is a spring and summer wonderland when wildflowers bloom and a palette of autumn color by mid-October.

Where: East High Street, about two miles east of I-75, in Lima.
Facilities: Campus facilities, which vary according to the time
of year.

For more information:

Tecumseh Natural Area and Arboretum, Ohio State University, Lima, OH 45801. 419-228-2641.

Index

172